Caroline Garland graduated from Cambridge in 1959 with a degree in English literature before going on to study psychology in America. Later at University College London her research consisted of ethological studies of play behaviour in the higher primates. Subsequent observations of mothers and newborns at St Mary's Hospital, Paddington, ended when her own children were born. Since restarting work she has concentrated upon the development and education of preschool children and is now teaching at a London school with the intention of becoming an educational psychologist. She has also trained as a psychotherapist at the Institute of Group Analysis and works primarily with students from the University of London.

Stephanie White graduated in 1963 with a degree in sociology from the University of London and joined the Tavistock Institute of Human Relations where she worked on various research projects concerned with management education, work organization and occupational choice. This work included a study of the careers of married professional women. In 1966 she published, with Everett E. Hagen, *Great Britain: Quiet Revolution in Planning*. She also worked on the Council for Children's Welfare until its demise in 1975. She gave up full-time employment when her first child was born. Since then she has been working on summer holiday play schemes in local playgroups and primary schools; and as a teaching auxiliary at the Natural History Museum.

Oxford Preschool Research Project

Children and Day Nurseries

Management and practice in nine
London day nurseries

Caroline Garland and Stephanie White

GRANT
McINTYRE

First published in 1980 by
Grant McIntyre Ltd
39 Great Russell Street
London WC1B 3PH

Hardback: ISBN 0 86216 006 5
Paperback: ISBN 0 86216 007 3

W 26349 /3. 3.85

British Library Cataloguing in Publication Data

Garland, Caroline
  Children and day nurseries.
  —(Oxford Preschool Research Project; 4).
  1. Day care centers—England—London
  metropolitan area
  2. Day care centers—Great Britain—Case
  studies
  I. Title   II. White, Stephanie
  III. Series
  362.7'1   HV861.G62L6

  ISBN 0–86216–006–5
  ISBN 0–86216–007–3 Pbk

Text set in 10/12 pt Photon Times, printed and bound
in Great Britain at The Pitman Press, Bath

Contents

For our families

Foreword by Jack Wrigley

In 1971, when a massive expansion of nursery education in Britain was proposed, there was relatively little easily available evidence to suggest how best this should be done. Consequently the Department of Education and Science and the Scottish Education Department initiated a programme of research on nursery education to answer practical questions about provision and to study the effects of expansion. The Educational Research Board of the Social Science Research Council saw the need for a complementary research programme concerned as well with some more fundamental issues which covered the whole range of preschool education.

The work was coordinated in the Department of Education and Science by a management committee on which the Schools Council and SSRC were represented. The original idea, that SSRC should concentrate on fundamental research while DES funded more policy oriented and practical work, proved too simple. What quickly emerged was a view that much of the fundamental work on preschool children had already been carried out. What was lacking was the dissemination of that knowledge and its implementation in the field. Within SSRC a preschool working group was given the task of commissioning projects, and the work of the Oxford Preschool Research Group, under Professor Bruner, reported in this series of publications, was the main element in the first phase of the SSRC programme.

Professor Bruner had already accomplished distinguished fundamental work in this field and was therefore well placed to make the point of the need for dissemination and implementation. Despite the many changes in the economic and political scene in the 1970s, the original gap in knowledge remains important and the results of the SSRC research programme will do much to fill the gap. In particular, Professor Bruner's work in Oxfordshire has great value for the rest of

the country. The publications of the Oxford Preschool Research
Group, together with the results from other participants in the
programme, will help give a firmer base on which to build for the
future.

Jack Wrigley
Chairman
SSRC Educational Research Board Panel on
Accountability in Education

London, 1979

Foreword by Jerome Bruner

This book is one in a series that emerges from the Oxford Preschool Research Group. Like the others in the series, it is concerned with the provision of care in Britain for the preschool child away from home and is the result of several years of research devoted to various aspects of that issue. There are few more controversial and crucial issues facing Britain today. The objective of the series is to shed light on present needs, on the quality of care available and on the extent to which this care meets these needs. The general aim is to provide a basis for discussion of future policy.

The studies have all been financed by the Social Science Research Council of Great Britain. They were commissioned in 1974, just a year or two after Mrs Thatcher's White Paper, *Education: a Framework for Expansion*, was published, at a time when it was thought that there would be a publicly financed expansion of preschool care and education in Britain. Since that time events have caught up with the enterprise and Britain finds itself in a period of economic stringency during which many of the hoped-for changes will have to be shelved until better days come again. Nonetheless, the studies are opportune, for careful study and planning will be necessary not only to meet present needs with reduced resources, but to shape policy and practice for an improved future service on behalf of children in Britain and their families.

Developmental studies of the past two decades have pointed increasingly to the importance of the opening years of life for the intellectual, social, and emotional growth of human beings. The books in this series, it is hoped, shed light on the practical steps that must be taken to ensure that the early years can contribute to the well-being of a next generation in Britain.

Jerome Bruner

Oxford, 1979.

Acknowledgements

Our thanks go chiefly to the children and staff in the day nurseries we visited. They not only made possible the research we report here, but made it for both of us a valuable and enjoyable experience.

Secondly we thank every member of the Oxford Preschool Research Group: Joanna Boyce and Sasha Metaxas for their patience in retyping innumerable drafts of the manuscript; our colleagues for their lively and helpful discussions of the many difficult issues involved; and in particular Jerry Bruner for the pleasure of his stimulating interest and encouragement at every stage of the project.

Finally, we want to thank Nicholas Garland and Roderick White for their great practical help and moral support.

1

Introduction

The period since the war has seen dramatic changes in our attitudes towards childhood, and in particular to very young children. On one hand there has been an increase in our knowledge about the relationship between upbringing and the emotional well-being of young children, brought about by such people as John Bowlby, Michael Rutter and the Robertsons in the professional field, and reflected more widely by Spock and Hugh Jolly. On the other hand there has also been an increased recognition of the important part that early childhood plays in determining the life-chances of the adult: children entering school at five vary enormously in their general grasp of language, their social and intellectual maturity and their capacity to profit from the kind of education our schools have to offer. Studies of the influence of social class and deprivation on educational achievement led to the setting up of Educational Priority Areas and the demand for an increase in the provision of facilities for the under-fives. Emphasis in national campaigns, however, has tended to be upon increasing the *quantity* of provision for the under-fives rather than upon the quality or kind of provision that should be made.

This book is one of a series concerned with current issues in preschool provision, based on research by the members of the Oxford Preschool Research Group. Our own volume has looked at some of the many types of day nursery that exist in London: we have tried to identify the advantages and disadvantages of each, and to explore some of the issues involved in current practice.

Changing views of childhood

It is difficult to appreciate how far our attitudes and beliefs are embedded in the times we live in. We, in the twentieth century, see infancy and childhood as well-defined periods of human existence, with their own institutions, patterns of behaviour and styles of consumption. It was not always so. One out of every four children in the eighteenth century died before it was a year old. In the mid-nineteenth century the proportion was one in six and it was not till after 1910 that as many as nine out of ten children survived the first year of life. It is not surprising, therefore, that interest in the development and upbringing of the under-fives is largely a preoccupation of the twentieth century.

During the eighteenth and nineteenth centuries, life was not easy even for those children who were sufficiently robust to survive the risks of infection in the early years of life. Families with young children have always been economically very vulnerable. Before the industrial revolution, work for the majority of families was home-based and children took their part in the family tasks as soon as they were old enough to walk. Even in the mines and in agriculture, where adults worked away from home, young children were employed at very early ages on simple tasks such as opening and closing traps in mine shafts, or scaring away birds from the fields. Equally in well-to-do families children were expected to adopt adult roles at a much earlier age than they are today.

The growth of urbanization and industrialization in the nineteenth century did not improve the plight of young children. Poverty made it necessary for women and children to work; women often returned to the mills within less than a week of confinement, leaving the new baby at home unattended. The break-up of the extended family when young people moved to the towns in order to find work made it often no longer possible to share the burdens of child care with relatives, as it had been in a more stable community.

The traditional alternative to leaving children unattended was the dame school, which was more of a day-care centre than a school as we think of it today. The 'teachers' were often elderly or invalid women who could not earn their living in any other way. For a few pence a week they would look after an average of 17 children aged between two and seven years old. The primary function of the dame schools was to provide a secure place where children could be left while their parents were at work, but most schools also included some basic instruction in the alphabet and reading. The early part of the nineteenth century saw a considerable increase in the number of these dame schools, but their numbers declined towards the end of the century with the establishment of State elementary education for children from three years upwards.

The first nursery school for young children in England was privately established in 1816 by the philanthropic mill-owner, Robert Owen, in New Lanark, for the children of his workers. Owen's ideas for the children's welfare would not be out of place in a modern day-care centre, with their emphasis on talking to the children, encouraging their curiosity, a good diet and plenty of fresh air. Unfortunately, the fact that Owen was an atheist meant that his ideas were rejected by the predominantly Church of England establishment and had very little influence on the development of state elementary education in the latter part of the nineteenth century. In State schools children were accommodated in galleries with rows of tiered seats, sometimes as many as one hundred to a room, and they were taught by rote. Jack Tizard and his colleagues (1976) estimate that the proportion of three and four year olds attending State-aided schools went up from 24·2 per cent in 1870 to 33·2 per cent in 1890 and 43·1 per cent in 1900. From 1900 onwards, there was a rapid decline brought about by the Board of Education's policy of separating nursery and elementary education.

The turn of the century also saw changes in attitudes towards the provision of day care. The original impetus for providing day care had been the need to look after the children of the poor and the women working in the mills. Apart from a few enlightened establishments like Robert Owen's, the emphasis was principally upon discipline, preparing children for a life of hard work and keeping them out of crime. Towards the end of the nineteenth century various philanthropists became concerned about the poor physical condition of children from the slums, and the emphasis shifted to a more liberal concern with the rehabilitation of sickly and undernourished children. It was not till the early twentieth century that the progressive ideals of the nursery movement took hold through the ideas of people like Froebel, Montessori and the McMillans.

Several day nurseries were established on an experimental basis in the latter part of the nineteenth century, and in 1906 the National Society of Day Nurseries was founded; but the principal impetus for the development of day care came from the two world wars. Day nursery places were provided for children of women working in the munitions factories and, in the Second World War, nursery centres were established to help cope with the problems produced by the evacuation of children from the danger zones.

However, situations which could be tolerated in times of national emergency were not sustained in peace-time. The importance of childhood as a separate estate was by now fully recognized and the duty of parents to care for their own children was a principle which could not lightly be renounced. In a joint statement of policy in 1945, the Ministries of Health and Education stated that the number of day nursery places should be reduced; children under two should be cared for at home; provision in nursery schools and classes should be made for children between the ages of two and five, and day nursery places should be reserved for those 'children whose mothers are constrained by individual circumstances to go out to work or whose home conditions are themselves unsatisfactory from the health point of view, or whose mothers are incapable for some good reason of undertaking the full care of their children'.

This is very much the situation that has continued to the present day. The number of state day nursery places declined from 67,749 in 1945 to 21,396 in 1965, and then increased slightly to 26,098 in 1975. Over the post war period the number of places in private nurseries increased dramatically from 6,893 in 1949 (when figures were first recorded) to 55,543 in 1965. However these figures are somewhat deceptive because they do not distinguish between private day nurseries and the private nursery schools which have flourished in the post war period because of government's failure to expand the State provision of nursery education. A more realistic estimate is that provided by the TUC Working Party on the under-fives (1976) which reckoned that in 1975 private day nurseries provided places for some 26,400 children (which is almost the same number that the state day nurseries catered for) but that the private nurseries were more numerous because the average nursery size was smaller.

The current situation

Despite the government's official policy of 1945 that the provision of day-care places should not be expanded, it is an indisputable fact that more married women are going out to work and, therefore, more children are being entrusted to substitute care. There are three sets of factors underlying this trend: demographic changes, changes in employment, and changes in social attitudes.

Women are marrying younger, they are having smaller families and their childbearing is spread over a much shorter period. At the same time they can expect to live longer, so that the proportion of their lives devoted to bringing up children is much smaller than it used to be. In the past, girls tended to have low career aspirations, not expecting to be employed for more than a few years before getting married and giving up work to raise a family. Those who did go back into employment after their children had grown up tended to find that they could be employed only in unskilled, low-status jobs.

With smaller families and the declining rate of population growth since the war, women have assumed a new importance as a reserve of labour in the economy. Whereas from 1851 to 1951 the proportion of women in the workforce remained stable at just under one third of the total workforce, since 1950 there has been a significant increase. Fifty years ago only one married women in ten worked outside the home, but in 1978 roughly 41 per cent of the workforce in Britain were women, and one married woman out of every two was working outside the home. The General Household Survey shows that by 1977 about a quarter of all children under five had mothers who were working outside the home either full or part time.

Why are more married women going out to work? Undoubtedly many go out to work for financial reasons. Recent increases in the cost of living and in property prices have made life harder for young families; more women want to have some degree of financial independence; and more marriages tend to end in breakdown – the numbers of one-parent families with dependent children increased from 570,000 in 1971 to 750,000 in 1976, an increase of 32 per cent. But there are other pressures which are just as important as the economic factors. Recent research (Ginsberg, 1976) has shown that many women of all social classes are 'highly dissatisfied' with being at home full-time as mothers, and that the lack of recognition which society gives to the tasks of bringing up children and looking after a home tends to lead to feelings of low self-esteem. The high incidence of psychiatric disturbance among women with children under the age of five is cause for concern (Brown and Harris, 1978). The last twenty years have seen the growth of many movements designed to ameliorate the position of women in society, ranging from voluntary self-help groups such as Women's Aid and the Preschool Playgroups Association set up in the 1960s, to Government bodies such as the Equal Opportunities Commission, and pressure groups such as the Women's Liberation Movement and the Campaign for Nursery Education.

So what does happen to the nation's under-fives? Official statistics show that more than a quarter of all children aged 0–4 spend at least some part of the day away from home. Of these children, rather less than half attend nursery schools or classes maintained or supervised by the Department of Education and Science, while the rest attend institutions which come under the supervision of the Department of Health and Social Security. The reasons for such a division of responsibility (between the DES and the DHSS) are largely historical rather than logical, and at a practical level are the source of much confusion and frustration. Figures for 1977 indicate that 0·8 per cent of the 0–4 age-group attended local authority day nurseries, 0·1 per cent were in local authority part-time nursery groups, 0·8 per cent were in registered private and voluntary nurseries; 11 per cent attended registered playgroups and 2·6 per cent were with registered childminders. This study is therefore concerned with the experiences of some of the 60,000 of the nation's children who spend their days in a day nursery.

The project

In 1975, Professor Jerome Bruner was invited by the Social Science Research Council to set up the Oxford Preschool Research Group, the task of which would be to focus upon preschool care and how it prepares or disables the young for later educational opportunities. Very early on in the project it was decided that the best way to discover more both about research possibilities and networks for dissemination of results was to work across a broad front in one locality, and Oxfordshire was chosen for this purpose. All the studies of preschool care for the under-fives except this one were accordingly based in Oxfordshire; but when it came to looking at day care it transpired that there were only three day nurseries in Oxfordshire and a handful of private nurseries, mainly in the city of Oxford itself. The decision was taken, therefore, to mount the part of the project concerned with day care in London, where the variety of day-care institutions available for study is much greater.

Having listed the various types of nursery available, we concentrated on visiting one of each type. Our final list included seven private nurseries and three State nurseries. All of them catered for children between the ages of three and five, but only three would take children under the age of two. The private nurseries included an all-day playgroup; a factory nursery; a hospital nursery; a university nursery; a 'community' nursery run by a local Community Relations Council and a private nursery run by a charitable organization. The State day nurseries included one which was experimental.

In any comparison between the State day nurseries and the private day nurseries, it is important to remember that those we visited were chosen in two different ways. When we were selecting the State nurseries we contacted the borough Social Services Department, explained the purpose of our project and asked them to select for us what they considered to be examples of the best practice in day care available in their area. When it came to private day nurseries we listed the different types of institution we wanted to visit (factory crèche, hospital nursery, community nursery, and so forth) and then tried to obtain introductions to appropriate institutions. There was not the same opportunity to choose only what was considered to be the best practice in any particular field.

We hope that this account of our work will provide a picture of what it is like to be a very young child who spends his version of the working day in a nursery; something of what it is like to work in a nursery; and some of the problems and issues which need to be considered when choosing, setting up, or working in a nursery. Decisions which at first sight may seem purely practical – the choice of premises, the hiring of staff, the choosing of equipment – are all constraints which have important consequences for the end product, the quality of the child's day.

Our approach to the study of the nurseries was two-pronged: Stephanie White interviewed senior staff in each nursery and Caroline Garland observed the interaction of children and staff. Every nursery we visited was given a great deal of forewarning of our visits, including, of course, the opportunity to refuse them altogether. The purpose of our visits was discussed before we arrived, usually with the organizer; always in the first instance by letter, and following that on the telephone as well. Every nursery was given the opportunity to ask whatever it wanted to know well before our arrival. Many of the nurseries we saw seemed used to having visitors, and accepted our presence with the minimum of disturbance, leaving us free to come and go as we pleased. For others it was not so easy. In every case, our initial visit was arranged so that the two of us met the organizer together. She would then usually take us round the nursery and introduce us to her staff, after which we began our separate investigations.

The interviews

The interviews were conducted from a detailed interview schedule which covered nine principal areas: the history of the setting up of the nursery; details of the service it provided; staffing; costing; premises; management; contact with other bodies such as social services and education; relationships with parents; and details of how the children were cared for. Two hours at a stretch was the optimum length for interviewing but the schedule took longer than this to complete. Wherever possible at least two visits to a nursery were made, but sometimes organizers (who are very busy people) were reluctant to set aside a second day for talking. On these occasions, the interviewer might disappear for a couple of hours and return in the afternoon, or stay and have lunch, or talk to other members of staff. We were conscious of nurseries' generosity in giving time to us, and tried to make the interviews as flexible as possible. Some were conducted in the room where the children were playing; but in some cases, where the organizer had an office, she preferred to withdraw to it – and this was in any case the place where she would normally be found. Even here there were plenty of interruptions, which often gave further insight into the issues being discussed.

The interview was conducted very informally. Note-taking during the interview was kept to a minimum to prevent it from interrupting the flow of conversation. There was no rigid order to the list of topics and the organizer was encouraged to expand on issues which were of particular interest to that nursery. Sometimes the interviewer was referred to other members of staff who had more detailed knowledge of particular topics. Occasionally it was impossible to gain information from any source. This was frequently the case over inquiries about how the nursery was costed, and occasionally over details of its inception and history.

The observations

The technique used, once the observer had become familiar with the layout of each nursery, was to sit on a child-sized chair in a corner of the room, and to record in a notebook what was seen and heard to happen in as great a detail as possible. Bouts of recording lasted for 20 minutes, after which the observer would stop recording for five minutes, and merely watch instead, to reestablish the context in which events were being seen. The focus of each twenty-minute session was an individual – more often than not a member of staff, but occasionally also a child if what it was doing seemed interesting, or relevant to that day's activities in that nursery. Recording attempted to avoid guesses as to the internal state of the observed (such as 'A was angry with B'), but confined itself to description of the actions and, where possible, speech; (for instance, 'A bending down towards B, shaking hand with extended forefinger near his face as she speaks 'You're a very messy boy . . .'). Shorthand symbols were used for many of actions occurring frequently, so that recording could keep pace with activity.

The amount of time spent in different nurseries ranged from a minimum of five hours to a maximum of nine. With the exception of the first nursery visited, where observations totalled seven hours, more time was spent observing in nurseries felt to be successful in providing a good standard of care than in those felt to be unsuccessful. There are two reasons for this: the first is that this observer found it increasingly difficult to sit and observe passively practice that she felt was bad. On one occasion, the unwritten rules of observation were broken by deliberately dropping a cup of coffee in order to bring to an end a scene between an untrained member of staff and a number of distressed children. On that occasion the priorities seemed clear; apart from this incident, however, the observer's ostensibly neutral role was sustained.

The second reason for spending more time in successful nurseries is that it is more difficult to define when things are going well (and even more so to see the reasons for it) than it is to determine when things are amiss. When an adult threatens a child with violence, or hurls its comforter in its face with a contemptuous remark, it is plain that something has gone wrong; but the outward signs of things going well may be no more, perhaps, than the expression on a face, or a particular quality to the noise in a room.

The story which we unfold in the subsequent chapters did not set out to be a critique of individual nurseries, nor yet a layman's guide to the dos and don'ts of nursery provision. We have tried simply to provide an outsider's view of the situation and to record what seemed to us some of the issues that might concern anyone involved with the care of the nation's youngest children: whether planning to set up a nursery, or hoping to work in one; whether looking for a place in an existing nursery for his own child; or concerned only with these same children after their day nursery career has ended – primary school teachers, for example, social workers and those who work in the child health services. A glimpse of the context of the earliest experiences of a child from a day nursery may help to illuminate many of that child's perceptions and attitudes, and make sense of what might otherwise seem irrelevant.

We are conscious that child care is an emotive subject and that feelings are likely to run high over what is considered to be good or bad practice. We feel some kind of brief personal introduction to the authors may help to provide the background against which the detail can be viewed. If the reader is forearmed with knowledge of our professional and personal stance towards child-rearing, we hope the findings decribed later will be more accessible and eventually of more use than if we had laid claim to an objectivity that is never entirely possible, either for researcher or reader.

We are both of us university-educated women with children of our own. Stephanie White trained as a sociologist and worked for five years at the Tavistock Institute of Human Relations on problems of industrial organization and career choice. Caroline Garland trained as a psychologist with a particular interest in the ethology of higher primates, and then went on to work in the field of child development and early education. We had both of us worked for some years before starting our own families and therefore had to face squarely the issues involved in abandoning our work when our children were born.

Our own styles of child-rearing have tended towards the democratic pattern characteristic of most of our contemporaries, rather than the considerably more authoritarian approach of our parents' generation. They may be reflected particularly clearly in what we have considered good practice in day nurseries, tending towards consideration of children as thinking, feeling individuals with attitudes and needs of their own that should not be ignored. Conversely and equally the result of our own family experience, we feel it bad practice to control children by public humiliation, threat of physical violence, or in fact any means too inflexible to take into account the varying needs of individuals (and in nurseries those needs do vary enormously because the children in nurseries come from a variety of backgrounds). Not many people would of course disagree with such a statement of ideals; but if the gulf between theory and practice can be great even in the home setting (as all of us are aware) how much more vulnerable are those who work in institutions with far greater numbers of children to care for; moreover children who, however close the affectional bond, are not in fact their own.

Critical though we may sound at times, we have both been struck forcibly by the tremendous demands made upon the adults working in day care, and by the isolation of their jobs. The inhabitants of day nurseries, adults and children, are more than most groups cut off from the larger world. Taking two young children to the shops can be tiring, but taking twenty is impossible. Yet it is such mundane experiences as buying a loaf of bread or visiting the launderette that provide the basis for many of the questions that the growing child begins to formulate about the world; and it is these questions in turn which provide for the adult, whether parent or caretaker, the starting point for so much of the stimulus and interest in the job of caring.

We begin with the practicalities: which were the nurseries we saw and how were they organized? This information provides the backcloth for the investigation of the world within.

2

The nine nurseries

Introduction

We visited nine nurseries in all, and as each of them will be referred to many times in subsequent chapters we felt it might be helpful if we were to provide the reader with some kind of thumbnail sketch which would help him to associate a name with a particular nursery. The three State day nurseries are described first, then the six private nurseries. Names and locations have been disguised to prevent identification.

Paul Street was a busy, noisy nursery run in old-fashioned premises on the edge of a redevelopment site. Many of the staff were West Indian and so were most of the children. The nursery's friendly and relaxed atmosphere owed a lot to the Organizer, who was outward-going and ready to take on anyone's problems. Her office was always full of people – parents, children, social workers and other members of staff looking for a word of advice. The children's rooms tended to be cluttered and shabby but relationships between the adults and children were relaxed and affectionate. Each afternoon a group of the older children were taken from this day nursery to their local state nursery school where they joined in the afternoon session. There were 63 children at Paul Street.

Church Road nursery had a curiously enclosed feeling about it, due, at least in part, to the fact that it was housed in an old police station complete with a cell block and an asphalted yard. It was more than just a place of employment for some of the younger members of staff, who knew very few people in London and depended on the nursery to provide much of their social life in the evenings and at weekends. The Organizer wanted the nursery to be used as a focus for the local community and much of her time was spent organizing social events, talking to parents, and lecturing to students on the role of the day nursery. The children were organized into groups which each had their own suite of rooms and seemed to run independently of each other for much of the day. Altogether there were 37 children.

Vienna Close. This was by no means a typical State day nursery. It had been set up as a testimony to an ideal and as a result was allowed certain privileges in terms of staffing and equipment. Its underlying principle was that it is futile to try to work with a disadvantaged child in isolation, and it tried to involve the parents of the children in the work of the nursery. Half the staff were themselves unsupported parents with children at the nursery, and of the other half a high proportion had training in child psychology and psychotherapy. Their philosophy of child care was much more coherent and explicit than in most of the other places we visited. The buildings and grounds were purpose-built and the nursery was used as a show place for the borough. There were 46 children.

Osborne Place occupied purpose-built premises in one corner of a large factory site. The layout and organization of the main room was reminiscent of a well-equipped nursery class and many of the activities the children engaged in were based on a similar programme. This programme was not devised by the nursery staff – who were all young and relatively inexperienced – but by the commercial company which the factory employed to run the nursery. Many of the 40 children were from India and Pakistan and had not learned to speak English before coming to the nursery.

Nightingale House was also a work-based nursery but this one was run as an integral part of a suburban hospital. The staff wore nurses' uniforms and used their nursing titles. There was a wide age range of children, with some under-twos, and fewer staff than in other nurseries of a comparable size. Physical needs were well attended to, but there seemed to be little time or inclination for cuddling and physical contact with the children – of whom there were 42.

Birkett Nursery was housed on the second floor of a university's large administrative block. Most of the children's parents were students. They were used to handling books and playing games like snakes-and-ladders or dominoes at home. They were generally a very self-reliant bunch of children – a characteristic which the staff recognized and were grateful for, because there were only two of them to look after 25 children. This nursery had separate morning and after-noon sessions and several of their children attended only part-time.

The parents were responsible for working out a rota amongst themselves to look after the full-time children during the lunch period. Though there were 25 places, there were also some part-time children, so that in fact the nursery catered for 31.

Wilberforce Nursery was a specialist nursery which put particular emphasis on language training for children of minority groups. Most of the staff were trained teachers; they were energetic and zealous in their efforts to stimulate the children both through activities in the centre and by an impressive programme of outside visits. However, the fact that preschool children need the opportunity to relax and to be mothered as well as educated sometimes tended to get overlooked. The majority of children at this nursery came from ethnic minority groups whose first language was not English. It was a very well-equipped nursery with a generous budget, and it catered for 23 full-time children, plus two part-time.

Runnymede Playgroup was run in a dimly-lit church hall on the edge of a redevelopment site, but the unprepossessing premises housed a particularly friendly, relaxed nursery. The Organizer was playgroup-trained and her helpers were all young mothers who knew each other and had children either at the playgroup itself or at the local primary school. The playgroup was only open during school hours. It was run on a shoe-string: parents helped by running fund-raising events, the staff improvised equipment for the playgroup, and they were all experts at bargain-hunting for everything from food for the children's lunch to paint and paper for art work. The emphasis on the formal aspects of education was less strong here than in some of the other nurseries; the staff seemed to get a lot of fun and enjoyment out of the children. There were 24 full-time children plus six part-time children, who were still in the process of settling in.

Marshall Day Nursery had been founded by a foreign charity but was expected to be self-financing. It had attractive premises in a suburban house with a large garden and sympathetic senior staff, but lack of funds obliged them to employ volunteers as junior staff on a nominal salary. These young girls only stayed for a few months at a time and few of them had had any experience of handling groups of small children; consequently their behaviour towards the children tended to be rigid and authoritarian. The two senior staff were aware of the problem but seemed powerless to do much about it. Marshall had places for 25 children, but there were only 17 full-time children at the time of our visit.

Organization

In general, the nurseries we visited saw themselves as providing all-day care for a group of children who would attend the nursery full-time for as much as 50 weeks a year. However there were various ways in which some of them sought to reduce the complexity of their task by limiting their commitment.

The first of these organizational options was to keep the size of the nursery fairly small. Most of the private nurseries we saw only catered for around 25 children. The two work-based ones were larger (Nightingale House had 42 children, Osborne Place 40), but neither was as big as the largest State day nursery, Paul Street, which took 63 children. One of the other two State nurseries (Vienna Close) was also built to take this number of children but they were understaffed at the time we visited them, so their numbers had been reduced to 46. The other State day nursery, Church Road, took 37 children.

From the point of view of staffing, the most important organizational option was undoubtedly that of reducing the number of hours for which the nursery was open. Runnymede was staffed by young mothers with children at primary school, so they closed each day at 3.30, and synchronized their holidays with the local schools. Wilberforce was mainly staffed by teachers so they also kept to terms and holidays, but their holidays were shorter and they had managed to operate a shift system so that the nursery was open from 8.30 a.m. to 6.00 p.m. The university-based nursery had a longer holiday in the summer to tie in with the needs of their parents, but even so they found it difficult to keep up the number of children they were looking after in adjoining weeks. Their day was organized on the basis of two independent sessions: 9.30 to 1.00 p.m. and 2 p.m. to 5.30.

The University nursery was one of the few nurseries which took many part-time children. In general, nurseries found that there were plenty of children to fill the full-time places and part-time attendance caused various administrative problems; it was often difficult to fill the spare time which one parent did not want, and it meant that planning the children's day was more complicated. Where all the children attend for a full day a variety of activities can be planned over the span of eight hours or so. A child who only comes in the afternoon may arrive during the other children's rest period or never have a chance to take part in certain activities, such as the directed play period which more often occurs in the morning when the children are fresher. Some nurseries did, however, use part-time attendance as a means of introducing new children or younger children to the nursery.

Of all the nurseries we visited, only three (Paul Street, Vienna Close and Nightingale House) had chosen to cater for the under-twos, and this was the area in which day nurseries were most clearly failing to meet the needs of the parents. As the Organizer of Paul Street put it: 'Nobody wants the under-twos, and this is the time when there is no break for the mothers – no playgroup or nursery class.' Even those State day nurseries which did take under-twos had very few places for babies or toddlers – they were limited to four children at Paul Street and seven at Vienna Close. In these circumstances, they did not take babies to enable their mothers to go out to work; they limited their intake to children who were at risk because of a breakdown in family relationships. The private hospital nursery on the other hand regarded caring for the under-twos as a much more routine affair. They only had two children which they classified as 'babies' but they had a further eight or nine under the age of two. They were prepared to take babies as soon as the mothers' maternity leave had come to an end, and indeed had six as yet unborn children on their waiting list at the time we visited them.

Admission to the nurseries

Only two of the day nurseries we visited (Runnymede and Marshall) had no special criteria for admission. Three of the others were attached to places of work and only took the children of employees or students (Osborne Place, Nightingale House, Birkett). The remaining four only accepted children on the recommendation of various welfare agencies.

Obviously the characteristics of the children being admitted to a nursery have some influence over how it can be run. None of the day nurseries we visited had very much choice over which children they admitted, but most of them recognized that it was important to keep a balanced community of children if possible. Two of the nurseries we visited had been set up to demonstrate the value of a particular style of child care (see Chapter 3, page 25) and they had a special responsibility to choose children who could benefit from that form of care. Vienna Close would only accept children whose parents were not working and would therefore be free to cooperate with the nursery. The heads of the various group rooms were always asked to discuss the list of children waiting for day nursery places in their borough and tried to choose children who they felt would fit in with their own group. Although theoretically they had more choice than most other institutions they had still achieved a situation in one room where they had too many boys in relation to girls. Although Wilberforce was trying specifically to cater for children with language problems they felt they had reached the point where they should not really take any more because their chances of success with the existing children would be reduced. Like Vienna Close, they also mentioned the importance of keeping a balance between the number of girls and boys at the nursery. Nobody seemed to find the girls a problem, but they were all wary of becoming over-weighted with boys. The staff at Birkett chose not to accept a proportion of local authority priority children, although they knew that, had they been prepared to do so, they would have qualified for a local authority grant. They felt that it would alter the composition of their group of children, which was very well-behaved and easy to manage, so they were able to run on a lower-than-average staff-child ratio. The staff at the work-based nurseries had least freedom of manoeuvre; their children were chosen by the personnel department and they just took those they were sent.

The turnover of children, once placed in nurseries, was fairly low. Only one of those we visited (Church Road) had a positive policy of moving children out once their family circumstances had changed. More commonly, if the family moved house a mother would travel quite long distances to keep her child at a particular nursery. Even where nursery classes are available for children aged three plus they are not usually taken up because the State education system only provides part-day care. Thus children normally left when they started school at rising-five.

Waiting lists at most nurseries are not just long, they are un-realistically long. We were quoted the case of a two-year-old at one of the state nurseries whose position on the list would not entitle him to a place for at least two years, by which time he would be ready for school! There are, however, means of manipulating the system.

In the case of the State day nurseries, admission seems generally to be preceded by a crisis such as a breakdown in the health of the mother or the child's becoming totally out of control, or by a marked deterioration in home conditions. Once one child from a family has been accepted it seems to be easier to get the other children into day care. And some children, initially admitted only on a temporary basis, for example when the mother goes into hospital, stay on and become permanent as soon as they have got a place. At the private nurseries, 'jumping the queue' is sometimes allowed on welfare grounds, but sometimes related to work requirements. Both the hospital and the factory nursery would put a mother to the head of the queue if she had a special skill that they needed at that time.

Sometimes a very long waiting list was no reflection of the reality of the situation. Typically parents would have approached the nursery and been told there would be several months delay before their child was admitted: since they needed a place then and there they had found some alternative form of care, but had not bothered to cancel their place at the original nursery. To illustrate, the Organizer at Birkett rang all the fifteen parents on her waiting list to try and fill the vacancies occurring in the next term. Of all those who could be traced, only two still wanted a place for their children. This kind of situation was also characteristic of Marshall, another nursery which catered for a high proportion of working parents as opposed to parents with problems.

Finance

Because the cost of places is so high, few institutions regard the provision of care as an open market, with places available to any mother who can afford them at the going commercial rate. Broadly speaking, this was true only at Birkett and Marshall in our group (though the latter did have some local authority places and would have liked to receive more grant support). These were also the only two nurseries we saw which had any difficulty in filling their places. When we visited them in 1976/7 Marshall's fees were £10 per week and Birkett's £7. Most State day nurseries operate, very differently, a closed system where the currency is *need* as defined by the social services team. The fees are means-tested and very few parents pay anything at all. There are many other people who would like nursery places, but they fall outside this tight definition of need and yet have no hope of being able to afford provision on the open market. Local authorities and other public bodies make limited recognition of this demand by providing subsidies for independently run day nurseries (such as Runnymede or Wilberforce). Some of the children attending these nurseries will have been given places because of social or physical handicap; so there is some balance here between the criterion of need and the ability to pay. The remaining day nurseries are those attached to particular institutions and set up specifically to meet those parent institutions' needs (as at Nightingale House or Osborne Place). These are generally subsidized, and the allocation of places at the nursery reflects the needs of the employer rather than those of the children attending the nursery. The fees were £3 a week at Osborne Place when we visited them and just 50p per week at Nightingale House.

It is unfortunate that the data we managed to obtain on the budgets of the nurseries was very limited. Only two of the non-state institutions produced figures which were accurate enough to permit comparisons. However, the budgets of these two are very revealing because they illustrate how unclear we are about the function of day care in society. Both nurseries were grant-aided but while one was run lavishly on the same kind of budget that a nursery school might expect, the other was run on a shoe-string, much more analogous to the position of a childminder who has to provide day care on the cheap. Wilberforce had an urban aid grant and Runnymede had a local authority grant. Runnymede was catering for two more children than Wilberforce, but they were only open in term times and during school hours instead of a full day. Nonetheless Wilberforce's budget for the preceding year was £29,000 whereas Runnymede was operating on £7,343. Rent and heating cost £3,000 per annum for Wilberforce and £288 for Runnymede; the equipment allowance for Wilberforce was £1,500, but for Runnymede a maximum of £30 per annum from their Social Services grant could be spent in this way. These are only two examples, but it is clear that there are vast variations between different day nurseries in the amount that they are allocated for their expenses. However, these differences are not clearly or consistently reflected in the quality of care which the children receive.

There is a great deal of ignorance on the part of staff in private institutions about the way in which their own particular nursery is financed. Some are run by extremely hardworking women who are battling against real financial problems to keep their nurseries going, and often subsidizing them out of their own pockets. Nurseries not specifically set up to cater for a 'distressed' sector of society appear to find it much more difficult to make ends meet. Birkett, Runnymede and Marshall were all trying to cover their own costs and finding it very difficult to do so. The staff at Birkett for example got free computer paper from the university for the children to use, but apart from that they only reckoned to spend about £5 per term out of petty cash on glue, paint, hamster food, tissues and all the other day-to-day requirements for the children.

The State nurseries, by contrast, seemed to enjoy a considerable degree of financial security. Their budgets were reasonably generous and the organizers took the view that if there was any accidental overspending on items such as heating or food this was likely to be sanctioned without trouble.

Premises and equipment

The range of activities which children at a day nursery can engage in is to some extent limited by the physical characteristics of the nursery and its setting. Where food is not prepared on the premises children cannot help with the cooking; if the nursery is a long way from the local shops or a park the children are less likely to be taken out regularly; if there is no outdoor playspace attached to the nursery, 'going outside' becomes an expedition that has to be planned.

Although all nurseries are subject to local authority regulations governing for instance space per child and children per toilet, the premises we saw were very varied. Two of the three State day nurseries were run in buildings which had been originally designed for (and used as) police stations; the third State nursery and two private nurseries were fortunate in having purpose-built premises; one private nursery was run on the two lowest floors of a large Edwardian house; one in a Church Hall; one in a converted supermarket; and one on the second floor of the administrative block at a university. However, although the newer buildings were very attractive, the attitudes and enthusiasm of the staff in some of the older buildings more than compensated for any deficiencies in the physical environment.

We identified three basic requirements which need to be met in any premises to be used for a nursery: there should be an outdoor play space; a large uncluttered area indoors, with space for unrestricted play; and a quiet room that the children can use for special activities.

The lack of adequate outdoor play space was something we came across frequently. Runnymede had only a narrow strip of tarmac about 15 feet long; at Birkett the children had to go some distance to get to a garden in a square; and at Wilberforce they could only play on a public forecourt which was not fenced off. This meant that staff could not leave any large equipment out and the children had to be watched constantly in case either they or their toys got lost. Nurseries that had only grassed areas found they were often unusable in winter time, and so the best arrangement appeared to be a combination of grass and tarmac.

The amount of space the children had indoors was undoubtedly an important factor. Without enough room children play on top of each other, interrupt each other's activities and find it difficult to hear each other speak. The staff at Nightingale House felt that their premises were rather cramped and this influenced the kind of activities that the older and more mobile children could be permitted, particularly as there were often crawling children in the same room. More uninhibited play had to be restrained – 'Batman' was banned. Although the premises at Runnymede were much older and more dilapidated, the huge amount of space available in the church hall allowed those children who wanted to play cowboys and indians to do so without interfering with anyone else, and the atmosphere was much more relaxed. Paul Street had perhaps the most unsatisfactory physical plan of all the nurseries we visited. All the children's rooms were interconnected, so that the rooms nearest to the front door were effectively a passage to the farthest rooms.

In every nursery the children's rooms had a very similar internal layout. They were generally divided by low cupboards into areas for different types of activity: a book corner, a dressing up corner, an area for messy play with paint and water, and so forth. But the appearance of the rooms was very different. Some, like Marshall and Osborne Place, had an almost clinical tidiness, plenty of purpose-designed furniture and few signs of the children's art work around. Others like Vienna Close and Runnymede were full of cheerful clutter: they had children's paintings sellotaped to the walls, home-made furniture and equipment improvized from old sheets and blankets. In part this may have reflected the amount of money available for equipment. If funds to buy a wendy house or a shop are there, there might seem little reason to improvize one. Yet the readiness to improvize and economize may also reflect a difference in attitudes to the children: to do with a practical concern for explaining how things work, how things are made; that it is possible to repair rather than only to replace.

The equipment available at different nurseries was also very similar: however attitudes towards the use of this equipment on the part of staff were different. At Vienna Close, for instance, the bulk of the equipment was out for most of the day. Short of out-right destruction, the staff's attitudes to it were tolerant: if a child wanted to use the bars of a doll's cot as a fort from which to fire upon his enemies that was regarded as legitimately inventive. At Osborne Place, however, when equipment was brought out from the large locked cupboard in which it was kept, the staff determined the way in which the children were permitted to use it. Similarly at Marshall those few basic books that were visible had been placed on a shelf out of the children's reach and appeared to be used as a controlling device. When the junior member of staff left the room she distributed books from a cupboard to the children and told them to read silently until she came back. When she returned she collected the books and put them away again out of sight.

A nursery's approach to its stock of equipment was reflected in the staff's approach to the children and their behaviour. Relaxed attitudes to equipment meant that children were permitted a lot of freedom over selecting and using toys, and that the staff's attitude to the children was as flexible and tolerant as it was to the equipment. At the other extreme, an over-zealous preservation of objects was reflected in an equally keen concern with control of the children and their behaviour.

The theme of this chapter has been diversity. We have seen that although the primary task of all the day nurseries was similar – to care for a group of young children five days a week for roughly 50 weeks a year – the ways in which they organized themselves to accomplish this task were very different. So far we have looked mainly at the *long-term* policy decisions which affect the day to day organization of the nursery: decisions about premises, whether to build or convert; decisions about budgets, whether to run a high-cost or a low-cost nursery; decisions about size, how many children to cater for, and of what ages; decisions about the service to be offered (full-time care for an extended day or more part-time provision) and to whom it should be offered.

This is the framework upon which the structure of the day nursery is built. Within this framework we can identify several unvarying requirements that are either inherent in looking after young children for long periods or that are conventionally considered to be necessary. They have to do not only with the nature of children (or what is thought to be their nature) but with the nature of adults and their reactions to being in charge of children for long periods at a time. One wants to feed them, to give them some time to rest (both adults and children), to give the children a sense of being with other children in a community, to give them some instruction assumed to be relevant to the next stage in their lives, and to give them some comfort and security. As we shall see when we examine the pattern of the nursery day in Chapter 4, all the nurseries struggled to meet these various requirements, but the ways in which they handled them were very different. The crucial dimension which we have not yet considered is the dimension of social organization: the nature of the relationships between the adults as they organized themselves to care for the children. Staff-child relationships have to wait till Chapter 5, but the management structure of the various nurseries we visited forms the central topic of the next chapter.

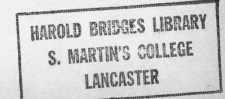

3

Nursery management

Setting up the nurseries

Education after the age of five is a universal provision in our society: it is available to all as of right. The State is prepared to provide it because it serves the needs of a modern democracy: you can't be governed properly if you can't read forms and regulations, road signs and notices; you can't become a useful citizen if you haven't learned how to handle money, how to use the postal system, and all the other conventions of our society. Before a child reaches the age of five, however, it is felt to be either unnecessary, inappropriate or even impossible for it to acquire the related skills. It is therefore not so easy to demonstrate the broader social benefits of day care, and that is why it has always been a partial rather than a universal service.

Historically, the most important reason for setting up day nurseries was to care for the children of the poor and women who were working in the mills. The emphasis fell on keeping children off the streets and discouraging them from bad habits. This concept of a service which is available only to a distressed sector of society is still with us today; it underlies the provision of State day nursery accommodation which, ostensibly through lack of funds, is only available to children at risk. Nowadays this service does not even cover the children of working parents; the three State nurseries in our study only took children with health problems, children on the battered register, children from one-parent families, or children from homes in danger of breakdown through poor housing conditions or ill-health.

The beginning of the twentieth century saw the rise of the progressive nursery movement which had an 'evangelical' attitude towards the provision of day care. This movement stressed the positive benefits to young children of an opportunity to mix with other children in a nursery setting under trained supervision. Whereas all the nurseries we saw in this project believed that they were doing something positive for their children beyond simply relieving the parents of the responsibility for their care, two of the nurseries we saw were established as 'model' institutions to demonstrate the values of a particular form of day care. Both were much more explicit about what they were trying to do for the children they cared for and both, in addition, had some commitment to research or evaluation. Vienna Close's founder felt that for state day nurseries simply to provide day care for children at risk was palliative rather than curative; she wanted to try and tackle the problem at its source by helping parents in their relationships with their children. The nursery was set up to explore the viability of different methods of staffing and working at a nursery: it provided an opportunity for six single parents at a time to be employed by the nursery and acquire an in-service training while still looking after their own children; and it put special emphasis upon working with the *families* of the children attending the nursery. One of the private nurseries, Wilberforce, had also been set up as an experimental institution, in this case by a local Community Relations Council, to demonstrate the need for positive intervention in favour of ethnic minorities. It had had two different organizers by the time we saw it, who interpreted the mission of the nursery in different ways. The first organizer wanted it to be a community-run nursery, but this interpretation of the project never really got off the ground. In the first place, the age structure of the surrounding estate was wrong; local children never attended it and it soon gained the reputation of being 'that black nursery'. In the second place, the Urban Aid Grant which funded it was paid to the Community Relations Council rather than to a local community group, so there was never any real scope for the community to decide what they wanted and how the nursery should be run. When the second organizer took over she reinterpreted 'positive intervention in favour of ethnic minority groups' to mean including a more rigorous educational component in the daily programme as well as coordinating the educational and medical services for the children in her care.

As we mentioned in Chapter 1, the period since 1950 has seen a dramatic increase in the involvement of women in the economy. Employers who had previously had no problem in recruiting and retaining female labour now found that their position was less satisfactory. Thus there was a straightforward commercial rationale behind the decision to set up nurseries for children of the staff at both the hospital and the factory which we visited.

Finally, there were three nurseries which were set up to meet a particular need for day care, but they were not established by the State or paid for by an employing organization. They could more reasonably be seen as an outcome of the growing belief that women have a right to some life outside the home, and that to deny them this right (if they feel they need it) may be to imperil their social and mental well-being, and thus that of their children also. Birkett and Runnymede both had their origins in self-help groups: the students set up Birkett for their own use and Runnymede was started originally as a half-day playgroup by a group of parents in an area of run-down housing. Marshall was set up by a foreign-based charity which had money to spend in England and a person on their staff who was interested in working with under-fives. From reading the national press they felt that there was a need for day nursery places which was not being met by State provision and they had also been influenced by reports of a spate of baby-snatching episodes.

Accountability

We found that the sponsors of day nurseries were not necessarily the people who were responsible for their day-to-day supervision. The State day nurseries were accountable to the Day Care Section of the local Social Services Department, but the accountability of the private day nurseries was quite a complex affair. Some were responsible to management committees, some to administrative officers; some were considered to be an integral part of the organization which had set them up, while others had independent supervisory bodies. In some cases the emphasis in supervision was very much on control: the responsibilities of the nursery staff tended to be limited and important decisions (including, incidentally, the right of the staff to give us their views of the nursery) had to be referred to the supervisory body. In other cases supervision involved more of a partnership, where nursery staff were accepted as equals and the supervising body saw itself as providing a service to the nursery.

The two work-based nurseries we saw were both subject to relatively tight control. Although Nightingale House was in a separate building from the hospital it was not run as an independent unit. The Matron was responsible to a Principal Nursing Officer who visited the nursery regularly two or three times a week. By contrast, not only was Osborne Place regarded as a separate unit from the factory but also the responsibility for running it had been subcontracted to a commercial firm which specialized in organizing nurseries. The day-to-day contact between the factory and the nursery was therefore very limited: the personnel department kept the waiting list and imposed strict health regulations on the nursery (the factory manufactured food) but it had no control over the nursery budget or its internal organization.

Runnymede was the only nursery we saw which was accountable to the parents of the children in its care. Several of the State day nurseries had tried to involve parents in the running of their nurseries but in their view they dealt with a group of parents who were unable to cope with the demands of managing a nursery, as these comments from Vienna Close and Paul Street indicate: 'They find it difficult enough to manage themselves,' and 'The mothers were ill-at-ease in evening meetings.' But at the Runnymede all-day playgroup there were regular meetings of all the parents and a smaller Parents' Committee which was responsible for running the playgroup. The smaller group discussed finance, outings and day-to-day problems; the larger meetings, which took place about every two months, were convened by the Organizer and discussed fund-raising and any problems which had arisen with the children. The staff got a lot of support from their management committee.

The remaining three private nurseries were each run by an independent management committee. In the case of the university nursery supervision was perfunctory and not very supportive. There was a large management committee upon which all the staff of the nursery and two or three parents were represented, but it met only once a term to discuss policy and items of general interest. The Organizer was accountable to a senior administrator but the delineation of her responsibility was very vague. She was responsible for liaising with the university's administrative departments for the solution of day-to-day problems, but lacked the authority to ensure that things got done. Similarly, she knew that the nursery was expected to be economically viable (and had been in debt) but she was very unclear about how the

fees she collected from parents were actually spent. Marshall and
Wilberforce were both financed by independent charities, but whereas
Wilberforce had a very generous grant, Marshall was expected to
cover its running costs and was subject to much tighter control. Both
nurseries were responsible initially to an administrator and then ultimately to a management committee which met monthly. The
management committee of Marshall consisted of three people – the
director of the charity, a trustee and a representative of the nursery.
Wilberforce was responsible to the local Community Relations Council, which was a voluntary body with members elected from the local
community.

The nature of the relationship between a nursery and its supervising
body is clearly crucial for the way in which the nursery will be run.
Two of the nurseries we saw (Nightingale House, Birkett) were treated
as offshoots of the organization which set them up; the remainder
formed part of a system of projects each with their own supervising
body. In the case of the State nurseries this form of supervision worked
well; for the private nurseries it was not always so successful. On the
one hand there are supervising bodies whose interests are too diffuse
for them to be able to provide proper backing and support for the
nurseries. This was certainly true of the charity running Marshall, and
Wilberforce also felt that the Community Relations Council knew too
little about young children to be able to advise them. On the other hand
there are the commercial companies who set up and run nurseries for
industry, hospitals, and so forth. These organizations should have the
expertise to advise the nursery staff, but what experience we had of
their operation seemed to suggest that their style of management
precluded the development of anything approaching a supportive
relationship. It is of course a very difficult sector in which to make a
profit; that is why their wages were slightly below average and their
staff often younger and less confident. The standards of physical care
and the educational aims set by the commercial company we saw were
high, but to ensure their achievement they had developed a tight
system of management controls which unfortunately tended to stifle
any initiative on the part of the staff. This kind of management control
system contrasts sharply with the loose federative structure of the
playgroup movement, where they attempt to work by example rather
than prescription.

Of all the private nurseries we saw, Runnymede appeared to have the most satisfactory supervisory system. Control was in the hands of the parents who made a genuine contribution to the nursery; but in addition the playgroup was very closely linked both with the Preschool Playgroups Association (several of the staff were on their courses and the Organizer was the PPA's local representative) and with the local authority through the Preschool Development Officer. This post was at that point unique to that London borough, in that it was an appointment made jointly by the Social Services and Education Departments for the supervision and assistance of any playgroups in the area. The staff salaries at the playgroup were all paid by the Social Services Department and rates of pay were related to whether or not staff had attended playgroup leaders' courses.

The importance of good support for nurseries from the Local Authority cannot be over emphasised. The provision in this borough for paying standard wages to playgroup personnel has meant that more schemes could be run; different kinds of people could be drawn into the field of caring for the under-fives; and their energies could be more wholly devoted to looking after the children in their care instead of running endless fund-raising activities. In the same way, the Local Authority playgroup shops which sold materials at cost price to accredited projects helped schemes to get off the ground and improved the service they could offer. Some boroughs had made constructive efforts to link up the various nurseries in the area and provide in-service training for the staff. One south London borough, for example, held monthly meetings for all the nursery organizers in the borough and a weekly craft workshop for nursery nurses. In other boroughs, nursery staff could spend so much time fighting bureaucratic tardiness and petty regulations that they felt their work was blocked and their energies misspent.

Management structure

The tasks which these nurseries were called upon to perform were basically very similar and yet the manner in which they organized themselves to accomplish those tasks differed greatly. The degree to which a nursery adopts a democratic or a hierarchic approach to organization is clearly governed in the first place by the kind of relationship it has with its sponsor or supervising body. Where for instance the emphasis is on control rather than cooperation, or where the powers of the matron are circumscribed by her supervising body, a hierarchical management structure is likely to develop.

In the two work-based nurseries (Osborne Place and Nightingale House) the Organizers had been relieved of most of their administrative responsibilities by the organization that was sponsoring the nursery. Their task was simply to supervise the staff looking after the children and cope with simple inquiries from the parents. Junior staff in these nurseries had very little autonomy and there were no staff meetings. All the staff at Nightingale House, including auxiliaries, behaved as the nurses they were. The Matron was responsible to a Principal Nursing Officer, and described the nursery as 'part of her empire'. All the staff were expected to take turns at looking after different age groups of children so that they did not become too specialized. At Osborne Place the Matron had even less autonomy. The Managing Director of the commercial firm which installed the nursery was at the head of the chain of command, and she issued programmes to each of the company nurseries, telling the matrons what they should be doing with the children each day of the week. Below the Managing Director was the Area Supervisor who was responsible for the conduct of several nurseries. The matron of each nursery received not only a programme for each week but also at least one visit from the Area Supervisor. Each week she had to send in a form compiled from the day book, covering everything from attendance and ailments to the poems taught that week.

The State day nurseries were much more democratically organized. The organizer tended to be fairly remote from the day-to-day lives of the children and concentrated on the administration and external relationships of the nursery. The children were subdivided into family groups and it was the leaders of the individual groups who were responsible for deciding how the children's day should be spent, under the general supervision of the two senior members of staff.

None of the private nurseries followed this pattern: with one exception, the children's activities were organized on a large-group basis for the major part of the day. Since most of the private nurseries were smaller than the State day nurseries this arrangement did not cause any administrative problems. Nightingale House and Osborne Place

were the only two private nurseries which were comparable in size to
the State day nurseries, and here, as we have seen, the problems of administrative complexity were resolved not by delegation within the
nursery, but by the parent organization taking over some of the administrative responsibilities of the senior staff. Though the children at
Nightingale House were divided into two groups for the major part of
the day, the division was based on age and ability rather than any form
of family group structure.

The four remaining nurseries (Marshall, Runnymede, Wilberforce,
Birkett) were small enough for the administrative functions to be
handled as part of the normal workload by one or more of the people
who were mainly concerned with looking after the children. At Birkett,
for example, there were only two members of staff. At Runnymede, the
Organizer was the only full-time member of staff and she therefore
bore the brunt of coordinating the nursery's activities. At Marshall, the
junior staff tended to be employed on only a three-month contract, so
there too the Organizer and Deputy Organizer had less opportunity to
spread the administrative workload. The job of the Organizer at
Wilberforce resembled that of a State day nursery organizer more
closely although her nursery was much smaller. The nursery was well
staffed and so could afford to release someone to concentrate on the
administration; but it also had a heavier workload. This was the only
private nursery we saw which had arrangements for home visiting;
they also undertook to coordinate educational and medical services for
the children in their care; and the nursery operated an extended day.

The existence of staff meetings, their frequency and the form they
take, provide some indication of the degree to which junior staff are
allowed to participate in decision-making at a nursery. Most nurseries
held regular meetings either weekly or fortnightly and some of them
were attended by outside consultants from the medical field. The only
nurseries which did not hold any meetings were the two work-based
nurseries (Nightingale House and Osborne Place), and Birkett where
there were only two members of staff. The meeting at Runnymede was
always held on the same day of the week, but not all the staff attended,
because some were part-timers. The Organizer felt this did not matter
very much because she worked with all the members of staff and could
act as a link in the chain of information. At Vienna Close, however, it
was felt to be very important that all the staff should be available to

attend the staff meetings: they were held once a fortnight after the nursery had closed, and a member of the domestic staff came back to look after the staff's own children. Although there was a shift system at Wilberforce all the staff over-lapped each day, and the five full-time members of staff also shared a long lunch hour. Nonetheless, there was a formal arrangement to hold a staff meeting on Mondays to discuss the week's programme. Since both these nurseries were committed to demonstrating a particular view of child care it was obviously important that there should be unity of purpose amongst the various members of staff. Although the staff at Marshall also overlapped each day their system of communication was more formalized. The people who came on the early shift planned out the day; any messages, for example from parents, were kept in a daily diary, which ensured that information was available to all the staff. Staff meetings were not an invariable event, but there was often a meeting on Friday during the children's rest period to review the week and share any ideas or information. Church Road had no regular provision for staff meetings to discuss the weekly programme of the nursery, and no meetings where all the staff of the nursery could meet. They did, however, have monthly assessment meetings for individual children in each family group, and these meetings were also used as training sessions for the junior members of staff. The staff in charge of each room also had the right to convene their own meetings (which they did about every two months) to plan future activities with the children and discuss any problems – tensions or disagreements – which had arisen between the staff. The Organizer and Deputy Organizer would attend a meeting of this sort only if invited, and even then would take a back-seat role.

Aims and objectives

In the first section of this chapter dealing with the setting up of the day nurseries we saw that day care in this country is not regarded as a universal service which should be available to all as of right. It is usually provided as a service to special groups in society either because they are seen to have particular social problems or because there is a local demand for female labour. We are, however, just beginning to see the setting up of more experimental children's centres in London, like the

Thomas Coram Centre and the Maxilla Nursery Centre, which aim to provide a universal service to a very small community in the immediate neighbourhood of the nursery.

Where day care is provided as some form of special service for people in need it is difficult for there to be an equal relationship between the parents and those who are providing the service. Wilberforce and Marshall, for example, were both set up by independent charities to serve the needs of special groups in society. They saw their job as being that of caring for the children and compensating for the parents where they were deficient. The State day nurseries also adopted a paternalistic attitude towards the parents: to a varying degree they each saw themselves as catering for the parents as well as the child, supporting their relationship and working with the parents to ameliorate the position of the child. Although there was no suggestion of social need in the allocation of places at the two work-based nurseries, Osborne Place and Nightingale House, these nurseries were heavily subsidized and so again the parents were placed willy nilly in a dependent relationship. There was also some evidence to suggest that the nursery staff felt it necessary to justify their existence by demonstrating that they could do more for the children than their parents could have done at home – the children at Nightingale House were toilet-trained much sooner that they would have been at home! The only nurseries which really accepted parents on an equal footing were Birkett and Runnymede. Both had been set up initially by groups of interested parents and had no additional mission. They saw themselves as providing an environment similar to that which the child would experience at home, but differing from it in some respects because of the large numbers of children present and the wide range of activities available.

In every place we visited, the staff stated two objectives: giving the children a stable, secure environment and providing them with some of the basic skills which they would need when they went to school. But the relative emphasis given to each of these objectives (and the degree of clarity with which they had been formulated) varied from one institution to another.

Vienna Close was the principal exponent of the view that the prime task of the day nursery must be to build up the child's capacity for handling social relationships. To this end, family groups of children should be looked after by a 'father' as well as a mother wherever possible; parents should be encouraged to spend time in the nursery and the staff should be willing to help the mother and child establish a better relationship if they asked for this help; the children themselves should be involved in any decision-making which affected them. Comments from the other State day nurseries echo the same preoccupations with the importance of social relationships. The Organizer at Paul Street said she wanted to give her children 'the feeling that people care about them' and thus 'to make them more ready for normal school life'. The Organizer at Church Road described her task as being that of seeing that 'the children we have and their parents are able to get whatever they need in the way of stimulation and emotional needs. . . . I am not only helping the child, but helping the staff to help the child, and helping them to cope with other adults.'

Wilberforce and Osborne Place, on the other hand, placed much more emphasis on the opportunity for compensatory education. Both of them had put a lot of thought into devising programmes of activity for the children, and Wilberforce took them on many educational visits. Although there were periods of free play in both of these nurseries, on the whole the children's day was structured and their activity was directed by the adults. Spontaneous child activity tended to be seen as a interruption of a set programme rather than a legitimate activity in its own right. Typical of this view of child care was the encouragement given to volunteers at Wilberforce to look for the purpose behind any activity being organized for the children: 'Do ask, because it is not just for fun; there probably is a reason behind it.' The importance of social relationships was not denied in this setting, but it was just seen as one part of what was taught, which was for Wilberforce 'the standard nursery school curriculum: social interaction, motor skills, reasoning, new experience, concept development and language'.

The playgroup philosophy, as expounded by Runnymede, took up a middle ground between the two objectives of education and fostering the development of social relationships. The Organizer felt that a playgroup should 'encourage children to do new things'. It should provide a stimulating environment and introduce them to materials to which they might not have access at home — such as paint, clay and dough. She felt she should try to encourage them 'to do all the things that happen at school', but this did not include formal instruction in reading and writing. She was also aware of the fact that life was not easy for some of her children. 'Small children have a very hard time, they are expected to grow up fast.' Their parents do not have the time or the skill to draw their children out. 'A lot of mums round here are frustrated, they need to work. And after all, you've got to face it, some mums need to be away from their kids.' The playgroup staff tried to give the children confidence, make time to talk to them and help them with their language, but they did not take upon themselves the same responsibility that the State nurseries took for looking after the parents as well as the children.

The staff's expectations of the children were also very different from one nursery to another.

One view saw the children as being basically sensible, reasonably responsible and capable of organizing themselves; they were encouraged to choose their own activities, participate in group decisions and help with the running of the community. Children at Runnymede, for example, were expected to help tidy the toys up or take a younger child to the toilet. The adults' caring attitude and concern for the children spread right through the institution, so that the children too were keen to help a newcomer or a younger child. At Vienna Close also the children were treated as potentially useful members of the community, as the following episode illustrates.

> The group leader announced his intention to continue building the observation platform. 'Anyone who wants to help had better come outside now.' Several boys ran outside, and were joined by some of the older boys from the adjoining group. The two male group leaders and a male voluntary worker discussed firstly how best to use the materials available (sections of elm log, railway sleepers) and then began to pile up the log sections. There was no specific attempt to get the boys to do particular jobs, but they joined in the rolling and piling of logs and the digging of a hole in which to sink a sleeper, as the opportunity arose.

The other view of children saw them as being basically unruly and incapable of sustained activity without adult direction, as a selection of quotations from the Organizer of Marshall illustrates.

> 'The children vary from day to day – sometimes you just have to let them run around and scream. . . . You make life difficult for

yourself if you make it rigid. . . . They get bored so quickly. In the afternoon their concentration has gone; you can't do anything with them.'

Whereas the expressed policy of this organizer was *laissez faire*, the Matron of the hospital crèche believed in civilizing her children from an early age: her staff started toilet training the children before they were one year old, they encouraged 'sensible food habits with no fads', and early practice in the basic skills such as counting, size grading, letter and colour recognition. Whereas both State day nurseries which took children under the age of two allowed the children themselves to choose when they were ready to move out of the baby unit and join a family group, the hospital nursery took this decision for their children. They moved them out at an earlier age, at about nine months old, as soon as they were onto three feeds a day.

In the factory nursery too the children were very closely supervised and controlled.

> While the water trough was being filled at the start of the day's play, the children were told to sit on the wall to wait. One child remained standing, and was told by the teacher returning with a bucket of water, 'Ajay I told you to sit on the wall to wait until I filled this up.' She brought a second bucket full, and the child was still standing in the eighteen inch space between the water tray and the wall, although not interfering with her task. The teacher reacted with, 'What did I say? Now sit on the wall! If you don't do as I say you'll have to do something else.' (i.e. not play with water). It seemed that, for the teacher, the point of getting the child to sit on the wall was to make him do something she had told him to, rather than that the act of sitting on the wall had any particular importance at this point.

Allowing the children to take the initiative is a hard thing to do; we saw fewer places where children were reasonably free to choose what to do than places where they were closely supervised and directed. Sometimes the high degree of control came from adults who found handling the children stressful and had very little idea of how to let the children spend their time (for example, the junior members of staff at Marshall). At other times the control came from people who were over zealous; they had designed an ambitious programme of activities for the children and were determined to see them through it.

In summary, all the nurseries we visited had two kinds of objectives for their children: social objectives, concerned with the capacity to handle relationships and the development of self confidence; and educational objectives, concerned with the development of those basic skills which they would need when they went to school and, in particular, the development of language. The relative emphasis which was given to these two objectives varied from one nursery to another. The way in which they were put into practice depended largely upon the staff's attitudes towards the children. In nurseries where the children were regarded as being basically unruly the emphasis in education was upon programmes of activity devised by the adults, and in social relationships the emphasis was upon control and learning to do what you were told. In nurseries where the children were regarded as basically responsible and capable of self-direction the emphasis in social relationships was upon the development of confidence and independence and in the educational sphere the children were given more freedom to choose what they wanted to do. There seemed to be less anxiety about the need to demonstrate what they had learned.

4

The nursery day

What is life in a day nursery like for the child? This is not a question that can be answered by listing the activities organized, or by scanning the day's production of paintings and toys from recycled household waste. These tell us what was done, not what it was like doing it. It is easy and tempting to assume that a 'product' at the end of the day has meant a busy and contented child. Many times this will have been true – but not always. In this example, neither adult nor children seemed to be enjoying their clay-modelling session.

Each child had been given a lump of clay, and made to sit round a single large table. The children pushed the clay about in silence, while the adult moved behind the chairs keeping up a running commentary on their efforts: 'What are you making? What's *that*? It's nothing, is it! You don't know what it is, do you! You're just copying. Well, make something – make a boat, make a car. Come on!'

The adults in a nursery may be aware of the value of a production to take home as an ostensible token of a day well spent.

In Nightingale House one morning, an easel and four pots of paint were brought into the under-threes' room. After one eager child had been told to wait, the nursery nurse then asked,
'Is Guy going to come and do a picture?'
'He says he doesn't like to do pictures,' answered another child for him.
'Don't you like to do pictures? Yes you do, don't tell fibbies!'
Another child wanted to paint but was told:
'Well *you* can't, you just mess everyone else's pictures.'
After a pause, Guy was asked again if he was going to do a painting, and he again answered no.
'Yes, you come on,' he was told, 'You only whine when you haven't got anything to bring home.'

Guy did not move. The children were sent one at a time to the easel and allowed to do one painting each, which was then hung up to dry ready to be taken home that night. Later the nursery nurse returned to her theme:

'Who's next? Come on Guy! You're always moaning you've got nothing to take home.'

Guy grinned but still did not move.

The nature of the experience, therefore, cannot be deduced either from the label on the activity or from the end product. How then can it be understood? To comprehend the subjective aspects of an experience as lengthy and varied as a child's day nursery career is perhaps an impossible task: children vary not only one from another, but also in themselves from day to day and even more so as year succeeds year, and their experience and capacities develop. The clay-modelling session described above would probably have been perceived differently by a shy three-year-old in his first week and a robust five-year-old on the verge of graduating to primary school.

Nevertheless, by sitting and watching what goes on day after day in a variety of nurseries, one begins to make guesses about the nature of the experiences that predominate in a particular setting, and tentatively to discriminate those that appear to enable a child to gain new experience or new skills at his own pace in a safe and orderly environment from those in contrast that are likely to make him feel that curiosity, exploration, and the risk-taking these involve are best abandoned.

Such guesses, though they may be informed by the experience of comparing and contrasting nurseries with each other, do not presume to do more than make a statement about the nature of the child's day: they do not attempt to identify the type of nursery most suitable for future academic attainment, or the development of social skills. Those are long-term matters for more detailed investigation. These observations are intended simply to give some glimpse into the world that the child inhabits for the space of the average man or woman's working week. We hope that our presentation in this and the following chapter will do two things: answer the specific question of what it is the child does during the day, and, equally, afford the reader some insight into the more difficult question of what life in a day nursery is like for the child. It is our view that these are complementary rather than alternative approaches to the problem: the external and the internal worlds, or the objective and the subjective realities, are neither wholly satisfactory without the other.

We begin therefore with a description of the order of events in a typical nursery day, before going on to describe some of the activities in more detail.

The pattern of the children's day

There are special problems associated with running a place which is open all day long. All the nurseries we visited had at least some routines at particular points in the day, such as circle time or story-time. They helped to break up the day into manageable blocks of time and to provide a recognizable structure for the children. Opinions were divided about the degree of structure that was desirable: some places like Wilberforce and Osborne Place had a detailed daily programme in many ways comparable to a school timetable; at others, like Runnymede or Vienna Close, the casual unstructured pattern was part of a deliberate attempt to recreate the kind of conditions a child experiences at home, where life is less predictable. However, the basic pattern of the children's day was similar in nearly all the places we visited. The nursery would open between 7.00 and 8.30 a.m., although the majority of the children would not get there till nearer 10.00. The two nurseries which did not open until after 9.00 (Runnymede and Birkett) were based upon a school model and were also closed for a large part of the school holidays. Although some of the children in State day nurseries would be given breakfast, this did not happen in any of the private nurseries we saw, even though some of the children at the hospital nursery, for example, had left their homes at 6.30 in the morning.

The first couple of hours in the morning, before milk-time, were spent in free play (though what was meant by free play differed from one institution to another, as we describe later). The range of equipment offered to the children in all the nurseries included sand, water, paint and clay or dough; puzzles, drawing materials, constructional games and lego, a wendy house or home corner; a climbing frame; and bicycles or scooters and balls for outdoor play. Obviously not all these activities would be available to the children on any one morning, but there would be a range from which they might choose.

At mid-morning the children would all be given milk and biscuits. Once a group of children were together in this way, the nursery staff often took the opportunity to read a story, sing some songs and nursery rhymes or talk about a topic of special interest. Two of the nurseries allowed the children to watch the BBC's *Playschool* after having their milk, but in general television seemed to be used relatively little.

The second part of the morning was often used for more directed activity. Sometimes this consisted of setting out a particular craft activity on one table, but sometimes it was organized more formally. At Wilberforce, the children had a twenty-minute music and movement session before being divided into age/ability groups for the next hour, when each group was taught something specific. Sometimes they used the same materials as in the free play session, but in a more directed way – for example, using the water tray to discuss sinking and floating, or hot and cold. Osborne Place also had an hour's 'lesson period', for which the children were divided into two groups by age and English-speaking ability. Two other nurseries we visited used a different system: a teacher (Marshall Day Nursery) or a play-leader (Paul Street) would be available in a small room to which groups of two or three children could go at a time. (At Marshall this was a privilege reserved for the older children.)

The supervision of meal-times was often left to the least qualified staff or to part-timers who came in specially to allow the permanent staff to take a lunch break themselves. One nursery, Vienna Close, was unusual in this respect in that they regarded meal-times as a special event in the day. They had a male chef who prided himself on his ability to avoid standard institutional food, and often in the summer, tea was packed up as a picnic to be eaten in some corner of the grounds. Family groups of children always ate together with their supervisors, and the nursery organizers would never intrude on a group at meal-time without being invited.

A rest period was compulsory for the children at all but one of the private nurseries, but none of the State nurseries insisted that all their children should rest. We felt that the rest period was as much an administrative device for giving the nursery staff a break as it was a necessary lull for all the children; the four year olds in particular seemed able to dispense with a formal rest period. Resting was very literally interpreted. The children were expected to lie on rugs or on their beds, generally without a book or toy even if they could not sleep.

In the afternoon the children tended to be taken out for a walk or to play outside if the weather was fine. Indeed, running about outside was clearly one of the most popular pastimes as far as the children were concerned. When given the opportunity the children – boys in particular – gravitated towards the large equipment: trucks and cars and climbing frames. The staff remarked that there never seem to be enough of them to go round, and the children often found it difficult to share the bikes.

Outside visits, and visitors to the nursery, provided some variety in the life of both adults and children at a nursery. Work-based nurseries seemed to manage less well in this respect than any others. The hospital nursery had no insurance to cover the children if they left the hospital premises, so they never went further than the big lawn of the hospital itself; and the children at the factory nursery were similarly confined to their immediate surroundings. The university nursery had recently acquired the key to a garden in a square, so their children were able to go out once a day, but they had not been on other outings in the neighbourhood. All the other nurseries took their children out quite often, either in twos and threes, when a member of staff wanted to go shopping or to the bank, or in small groups to the local park, playgroup, library, or swimming pool; or occasionally on more organized outings to a farm, or a museum; even once on a camping trip.

At every nursery we visited, activities tended to tail off towards the end of the day, when both staff and children were tired. Although the nurseries might be open until six o'clock, parents often came to collect their children from three o'clock onwards, and not many were left there till the nursery closed. Nonetheless, for many of these children it was a very long day away from home, longer than they would experience when they went to school at five.

Let us now look more closely at what some of the activities mentioned actually involve.

Free play

Free play is a type of activity that most day nurseries include in their
daily programme at some point or another. However, what different
nurseries describe as free play ranges from the totally supervised and
carefully structured to the totally uncontrolled. This last was perhaps
best exemplified by Marshall Day Nursery which said, 'We just tip the
drawers out onto the floor and let them do what they want.' (This
nursery – very unusually – also let the children play out-of-doors unsupervised.) The two nurseries where adults were the least concerned
with what the children did during 'free play', giving it a very minor role
in the daily rota, were also the most structured with their lessons, and
had the most rigid format to the day. In Wilberforce, for instance,
where free play occupied only the early part of the morning before all
the children had arrived, often only one adult was in the room with up
to 25 children at a time. In these two places, the impression was that
the staff had made a clear distinction in their minds between play
(= fun) and work (= not fun), and considered their own role to be
specifically work-orientated. The children needed an adult with them in
order to work; what they did on their own was then felt to be by definition 'play', and less valuable than work. For some nurseries the subtle
relationship that can exist for a child between playing and working,
such that either can be equally serious in intent, was either a mystery
or an irrelevance.

Quite a different view of 'free play' was found at Runnymede, which
functioned as an all-day playgroup. Here, no distinction was drawn
between play and work, with the result that the children were permanently free to choose between a number of activities. However, once
a particular activity had been chosen, there were certain constraints
upon the way in which it might be pursued. Some carried with them
fewer restrictions than others: building with bricks obviously gave
more room for individual variation and less need for supervision than,
for instance, did tissue paper collage. When this activity was provided,
a good deal of intentional structuring was included.

On one table, pieces of paper were laid out with circles drawn
in pencil upon them. An adult sat at the table with a child and
demonstrated to him what was to be done. 'We're going to make

a football. Shall I show you how to do it? You take a bit of paper like this . . .' (taking a small square of coloured tissue paper out of a box) 'and then you do this' (crumpling the paper gently in her fingers) 'like this, all scrumpled up. Then you put a bit of paste on it,' (dipping the edge of the tissue paper ball into a wide-necked pot of paste) 'not too much! Then you put it all round the edge like this,' the adult concluded, pressing the tissue down onto the line drawn on the paper in front of the child. She did two more such pieces, placing them close to each other and then watched the child do one himself. 'I can leave you to do that now and I'll be back in a little while to see how you're getting on. That's very good now, isn't it.' She then left the table.

Yet it is clearly hard to tell how much impression tuition will make upon its recipient. In this case, the adult's words perhaps had more effect than she had intended, since a second child arrived at the table, and after watching the first for a few moments, started a 'football' himself. However, he put his piece of tissue into the middle of the circle; which led the child who had received the original instructions to lean over without a word and move it outward to the pencilled perimeter of the circle. There was no reason why the collage should not have begun from the middle and spread outwards, but this had not been part of the original instructions.

Thus the amount of structuring by an adult might affect different children quite differently; there was no obvious correlation between intention and effect. It is easy, merely because one is an adult, to give the impression that there is a 'right' way to play simply by offering a comment on the way a child is behaving. Sometimes indeed, there does seem to an adult to be a right way of playing with a toy, and this can both be inappropriate, and have a restricting or discouraging effect on the child's own play. In one nursery, a child was building, knocking down and rebuilding, a series of towers that he constructed from a pile of nesting cups. For him, the point of the game seemed to be the variety of ways in which this could be achieved, but for the adult the point was that every cup should be used in its correct sequence. Thus the boy was told twice 'You've still left one out.' Eventually, perhaps discouraged, he said he had had enough and was told to put it away; he spent five minutes laboriously putting it together 'properly', but when he handed it to the staff member she took it from him with no change of expression, saying simply 'Is that all?' before she put it away.

A nursery that made a clear distinction between play and work, such as the one where children were felt to be playing only when allowed to engage in a free-for-all with every toy dropped before them onto the floor, might well have regarded tissue paper collage as 'work'. We do not intend to argue over terminology, but it is worth thinking about the differing effects upon a child of being told that what it is doing is play, or is work. Is a painting, for instance, work or play? The implicit value attributed to an activity by a member of staff is all too easily conveyed by the label she chooses to attach to it; both 'play' and 'work' in our society are value judgements.

Every nursery, however, liked to see the children occupied. In several this was made quite explicit.

> At Nightingale House: 'What are you going to do, Sharon? Are you? All right. Go on then, you find it yourself. What about you? Have you finished your painting? Are you going to play with the pastry now? All right then, go and wash your hands, and wash the brushes . . .' 'What's this picture of?' 'A monster.' 'A monster! Very nice, now go and wash your hands.'

> And in Runnymede we heard: 'Come and be busy,' or 'Shall we go and be busy?' several times, accompanied by the adult's taking a child by the hand and leading it towards the smaller room.

Sometimes the directive to be occupied could take the form of a rebuke:

> '*Make* something with the bricks, come on, build something.' (Nightingale House)

> 'Sit down and make something – you never do anything, do you.' (Church Road)

In most nurseries, once a child was engaged in an activity, it could be fairly confident that the amount of adult attention it would receive was dependent upon the activity it had chosen. In fantasy play, it was rare for an adult to intervene unless the noise level grew too high for comfort; it seemed to be tacitly understood that it was inappropriate for a child's fantasy world to be entered by an adult. When a child was sitting at a collage table, however, an adult was invariably there too, at first to instruct, and from time to time to help, monitor and advise.

This raises the question of whether children chose particular activities because of the likelihood, or the lack of it, of an adult's being there too. It was our impression that girls were more likely to engage in activities in which adults were present, and that boys showed an equal tendency to engage in unsupervised activities. Thus during a morning of free play, the boys would spend more time than the girls on the larger pieces of apparatus, or in fantasy games involving running, shooting and climbing, and girls would spend more time than the boys sitting at tables engaging in puzzles, bead-threading, collage, etc. (Painting was equally popular with both sexes, as was play with water.) We could not, of course, tell whether the boys were attracted towards the active games or away from the adults; and similarly whether the girls were attracted towards the finer motor skills or towards the adults. However it would seem worth attempting to provide a 'balanced diet' of activities with or without adults for both sexes, bearing in mind the tendencies of each.

Fantasy

Most nurseries either created or left some space in the nursery day for the children to play with no adult intervention at all. Often this resulted in some fantasy play, although the amount varied. In other nurseries there was very little adult cooperation in terms of providing the necessary conditions – time, space, a degree of privacy, a few props in the shape of a dressing-up box, a wendy house or a shop, and 'at the minimum, no strong disapproval of make-believing' (Garvey, 1977). However, in one nursery mainly populated by Asian children it was virtually ruled out altogether because the staff had imposed a ban upon the children's speaking any language but English. It is not of course possible to eliminate solitary fantasies and no doubt these play their part in every child's day, but games of Mothers and Fathers, Bionic Man, Batman and Robin, Doctors and Nurses, need more than one player, as well as some degree of cooperation from the adult world.

Yet providing the necessary conditions is no guarantee that fantasy will flourish. In Church Road and Birkett, possibly for different reasons, there was little fantasy play seen and it was interesting to speculate upon the possible reasons for this. In the first nursery there were marked differences between two separate family groups in the amount of fantasy play. In this instance, it was possible that the greater amount of fantasy in one family group was related to the distance that existed between the children and adults. Here the staff acted primarily as setters of limits to behaviour (noise, aggression, mess) and within these limits children were free to do as they liked. In the other family group, in contrast, the staff acted as innovators and stimulators, and more significantly as participators and allies. 'Let's all ...' was a typical preamble to some activity, rather than 'Why don't you ...?' Unintentionally, the reduced emotional distance between adults and children in this setting may have served to reduce the amount of fantasy. It is undeniably difficult to become immersed in a game in which you are an adult if there is a real adult wanting to play too. Although Tea-time, Going Shopping and Telephoning, all favourites with the younger children, are played with gusto with adult partners, the games favoured by the older children such as Mothers and Fathers, Doctors and Nurses, even Bionic Man, were marked by, as it were, the absence of inverted commas: they became a fantasy in which objective reality was temporarily suspended, rather than a game of Let's Pretend, in which the actual and the assumed reality existed side by side.

Little fantasy play occurred in the university nursery, also. The children here were a highly articulate group, and would talk imaginatively together while sitting round a table engaged in some activity such as cutting and sticking, but there was less acting out of this material than in other groups. It may have been that their verbal skills eliminated some of the need for action; it might also have been that the unusual amount of television watched by this group reduced the amount of fantasy – either by leaving them less time for it, or by providing vicarious fantasies which to some extent absorbed the children's own material.

The psychoanalysts have much to say about the significance of fantasy play. Whether or not they are right in their interpretation of specific instances is of course open to question, but it is clear at the very least that: 'It is perhaps one of the most complex kinds of play conducted in childhood, since it is likely to encompass most if not all of

the resources at a child's command and to integrate them into a whole.'
(Garvey, 1977). Without going so far as to suggest a specific need for
fantasy within a child's day, such an integrative function must give it an
important place in any hierarchy of opportunities to be made available. It
does not require much in the way of adult effort to provide the opportunity
for fantasy play, and we felt that the nurseries that did so were in less
danger of missing out a potentially productive and certainly pleasurable
ingredient of the day than those that filled every moment of the child's time
with well-organized activity.

Structured play, or 'doing something'

In some nurseries the most structured activity to be seen was
equivalent to what another nursery might have designated free
play – an activity chosen by a child from a selection produced by an
adult, and played according to adult rules. However, the instances of
tissue-paper collage already quoted shows this kind of activity at its
most flexible: adult rules could be altered by a child who did so inven-
tively. The activity had been announced as 'We're going to make a
football.'

> Later in the session, a little girl had begun to go round the
> upper part of the perimeter of the circle, but she changed her
> mind half-way, and by adding tissue-paper balls below to form
> eyes, a nose and a mouth, changed it into a woman wearing a
> multicoloured tissue wig. 'It's you!' she said to the adult at the
> table, who went quite pink as she replied 'Oh, is that me? Oh
> that's lovely! Isn't it lovely, Linda!' to the playleader.

Not all adults took so well to innovation. At Marshall Day Nursery,
the Deputy Matron was supervising a painting session.

> She drew with a compass four or five identically-sized pencil
> circles on each piece of paper, each child being given one such
> sheet. The children were told to fill in the circles with colour as
> they were to be pictures of balloons. They were told to keep
> within the lines; praise was given for neatness and speed. One
> child painted all her balloons black, but was told, gently, to wash

her brush and to do the final one in a different colour. 'I should do it in yellow, or it won't be very bright.' A boy who wanted to turn his circles into an owl was told, 'No don't do that, because they're really balloons.'

In the first example, it can be seen that the adult was in fact teaching a *technique* (in this case, tissue collage) and that experimentation with that technique was not merely tolerated, but applauded. At Marshall Day Nursery, however, it seemed on this occasion that the adult had a very clear idea of the finished product and was unable to tolerate deviations, even in colour.

More frequently, however, during structured activity a child was given no choice; the activity was chosen, provided and supervised by an adult. The clearest examples of this approach were seen in Wilber-force, where the children were divided into age/ability groups for part of the morning. This group was making dough. There was a lot of activity in this session, although the language was provided entirely by the adult.

'We're going to make some pastry here today, and then we're going to play with it. Now who can tell me what we need to make pastry? Yes, we use a bowl; what else do we need? Well, I'll tell you – we need flour and we need water. And we need some aprons or we'll get all messed up, won't we.' The teacher then helped the children dress themselves in plastic aprons. 'Don't make that horrible noise, Ben, it gives me a headache. Sally, would you like to tip some flour into the bowl to make some pastry? Katy, here's some oil – would you like to tip that in? Here's some salt. The salt's to make it stay good; it stops it from smelling. Here's some yellow colour. Katy, can you show me something yellow on the table? Here's the yellow colour. Would you like to start mixing it with your hands, round and round, so the water and the colour and the flour and the oil all get mixed up. . . . What does it feel like? Soft! Yes, soft! Is it wet or dry? Do we need more water in? It (the vegetable colouring matter) looks orange in there (holding up the bottle) doesn't it, but it'll be yellow when it's all mixed up. Is it mixing up nicely? Is it feeling like pastry? . . . I think we need a bit more water in, don't we, to make it a bit wetter; it's a bit too dry. (To the child who was mixing the

dough with his hands:) Do you want to get your hands clean? Go
and wash them then. Is it all sticky? Yerch, it's all sticky. Can I
have a go? Can I finish it off now, or we won't have time to play
with it. It takes a long time to mix, doesn't it?' She finishes
kneading the dough herself, until it's a proper consistency for
play. 'Here – shall we have a bit of dough each now? Would you
like a bit to play with, Ben? Here's a bit for you, Wendy. What
are you doing, Carole? You've rolled it out, haven't you; you're
making shapes.'

It is possible that an adult less intent upon instruction might have
found herself with a group of children more able or willing to articulate, however hesitantly, their own discoveries.

Still more structured was a finger-painting session observed in the
factory-based nursery. Waiting children queued, while two at a time
were permitted to sit at a plastic-topped table while the paint was
spread out in front of them. They were told to make patterns in it with
their fingers, a process which took them a maximum of two to three
minutes. The teacher then, herself, applied a piece of paper to the
pattern, rubbed it down and peeled it off, remarking to the individual
child as she lifted it up again, 'There, that's a pretty pattern isn't it?
Now wash your hands and go outside.' Their places were then taken
by the next children in the queue.

Of course, gauging the amount of intervention appropriate or
desirable in the nursery setting is a skill which approaches an art.
Moreover, fashions in education change, as much in the nursery world
as in the secondary school, and what one generation might consider
over-intrusive another would feel was dangerously *laissez-faire*.

Story-time

All nurseries had a story-time, or spent some time each day in reading
to the children. The form it took depended on the number of children
involved. Where story-reading was used as one of a number of
pleasurable ways in which adult and child might interact, it was initiated by the child, who approached the adult with a book with a
request to 'read me this story'. Sometimes one or two other children
would then gather to listen.

More often stories were chosen by adults to be read to a larger groups, where the potential intimacy of the event was diminished. Then it served a different purpose: that of a structured activity. This instance came from Runnymede.

> The reader sat on a chair looking at a group of children who were on a mattress facing her. However, before they got further than the first sentence, the story was interrupted for Kleenex to be found and two noses to be wiped. A moment later, the story was held up again as a girl was taken into the small room with the remark that the reader was 'sure she isn't going to behave'. When the story finally got under way, and the children were quiet, the procedure was for the adult to finish reading a section and then hold up the book for the children to look at the accompanying picture.

In contrast was the setting at Vienna Close, where the reader sat on the mattress among the children, so that they all looked at the book together. Not only did this mean that words and pictures were integrated, but that looking at the book was an experience that was shared simultaneously by adult and child. Although there is no way to be sure that this increases the degree of the child's participation in the event, it seemed that the alternative, as practised by the reader at Runnymede, must, by the physical distance of the children from the book and the way in which the adult held up some and not other pictures, have increased the likelihood of the children's thinking of reading as fundamentally an adult activity. No child asked for the book at the end of the story, nor was it offered, in vivid contrast with the tussle over which child was to have the book at the end of the session in Vienna Close.

Sometimes, the primary significance of story-reading was lost, and it became merely a device for controlling the group: for keeping it motionless, quiet and clean – for example before lunch at Church Road.

> A lot of time was spent in getting the children to behave as required before the story could begin. 'Cross your legs – come on. Come on, Gary, like Adrian. Sit nicely or you'll have to sit on the table. Gary, SIT STILL.' Both vocabulary and sentence structure in this version of *Beauty and the Beast* were too com-

plex for this age group, and the story, which lasted for 20 minutes, was read at a rate which attempted to preclude interruptions. Pictures were rarely turned so that the children might view them, and the only language that occurred outside the written word were occasional reprimands from the reader to wrigglers.

Nowhere did we hear a story told, as opposed to read, unless it was by those professionals upon television's *Jackanory* (who are, of course, reading from the invisible teleprompter). Telling a story is not these days an alternative to reading, but there seemed no apparent reason why it should not be a pleasurable addition to experience with books. Adults seem to have lost the confidence that children have in abundance when it comes to inventing, and telling, a story.

Lessons

Some nurseries took structured play even further and devoted a part of the day to activities that were felt to be specifically educational, or work as opposed to play. As we have already said, these were the nurseries that attached least value to play, giving it a relatively unimportant part in a highly structured day. In 'lessons', specific information rather than skills was imparted, and through direct instruction rather than by providing an opportunity for discovery.

By far the most common material subjected to this routine was number and colour, probably because it is easy to test whether or not it has been learned.

> In Nightingale House, after the ritual of handwashing and table-wiping, the children sat at a bare table; some waited for ten minutes until the last child had been scrubbed and dried satisfactorily, kept in their places with repeated requests to sit *still* and be *quiet*.
>
> 'We're going to do colours.'
>
> 'Why?'
>
> 'So you can learn them, that's why! Now, I think we'll start with red. Who's got red on? Stand up anyone with red on. Yes, Stephen?'
>
> 'Yes, Stephen's got red trousers, good, sit down.'

A child who said that his trousers were red when in fact they were blue was told not to be silly.

In another nursery, numbers, colours and the days of the week were being taught to the oldest children in preparation 'for school'. This prompted a small Asian boy to burst in out of turn with what for him was important about that approaching experience: 'My Daddy's dead, but I've got a grandfather and he's going to take me to school.' 'Is he?' responded the teacher, and continued asking the children to recite in turn 'It-is-Wednesday-the-thirtieth-of-June-hot-and-sunny.' Correct naming and classification was the main emphasis in Marshall's 'lessons'. The teacher was delighted when a small girl remembered that the name for knives and forks and spoons was 'cutlery'.

The children in nurseries where such information as numbers and colours was acquired along the way, rather than imparted during formal sessions, did not appear to us any less competent than their contemporaries. It is worth considering the notion that obedience, or doing what one is told when one is told to do it, is in fact the primary lesson being taught during 'lessons'. However, to have learned it too well too young is a possible handicap when the child eventually finds itself in primary school where the 'good' children are those who, willy nilly, receive the smallest share of the teacher's attention; the bright, the slow and the naughty all come higher up the list.

Attention span

We felt that the development of the individual child's attention span was one of the most important opportunities a nursery could provide. One of the problems with formal lessons was that they make it difficult to determine the length of a child's natural attention span. During lessons, not only the subject matter, but the beginnings and ends of activities are determined by adults. In theory a lesson prolongs the attention span, or might be capable of doing so with considerably older children; with the under-fives, it is likely to miss the target altogether.

Many of the young children observed in these day nurseries had a clear sense of the appropriate endings for activities they were engaged in and, given the chance, would 'complete' an activity in however perfunctory a manner. One child turned rapidly through the remaining pages of a book until the end was reached before joining the rest of his group at circle time. Others completed a Lotto card for themselves after the game had been won and ostensibly was over. Usually, a chance to achieve completion in the child's own manner is given by an adult's warning that clearing-up time is approaching.

Occasionally the considerable ability of a child to stay with an activity was disrupted, either by older children, or even by an insensitive intervention from a staff member. In Paul Street, a three-year-old, among the noise and bustle of the nursery, attempted to concentrate upon a task she had evolved for herself.

On a table, a puzzle consisting of a simple picture of a farmyard scene was laid out. Each puzzle piece consisted of an entire animal which could be removed from the board by means of a small knob. Building blocks and another puzzle were out on the same table. Several pieces of the farm had already been removed although some were still in place. Another younger girl (Fiona) came in and sat at the table. She picked up one of the farm animals and looked at the partially completed board. She attempted to fit the piece into the board, but was unsuccessful because she had selected the wrong hole. While she pushed and fiddled at the hole with the puzzle piece, her eyes were on the girl playing with model farm animals at another table. She chose a different piece and this time fitted it correctly into the board. This small success appeared to give her some impetus and she chose another piece, this time scanning the board carefully to select the appropriate hole. She kept her gaze on the board. She succeeded after a false try in fitting it too into its place; she then succeeded in fitting three more pieces. At this point, instead of completing the puzzle, she removed *every* single animal piece by its peg, laying them out before her.

While she attempted, with her fresh start, to fit the first piece, the student arrived beside her, sat down abruptly and asked her the name of an animal figure which she held up. Fiona smiled faintly as she answered but did not look at the student, continuing to shift her gaze between the piece she was holding and the board. After one and a half minutes the student got up and went as abruptly as she had arrived. Fiona's attention was shifted away from the puzzle; she watched the student go, gazing after her and sucking on the puzzle piece in her hands. She got up and moved to another seat and removed all the pieces from the other puzzle at the same table. She then attempted to refit them (it was a simpler task than the earlier one), but had reverted to her earlier unfocused behaviour: her hand tried to fit the piece in the hole, but her gaze was on the other children in the room. The student reappeared in the doorway and asked, 'Fiona, shall I put your dolly to bed?' moving to the home corner. Fiona got up and went over to her, watching the student tucking the doll up, but she neither helped nor commented. After a moment she went outside.

Although it is possible to identify the immediate factors that prevent a child from focusing on an activity, it is of course harder to see what it is that enables it to concentrate. Frequently, a setting that allowed a child's attention to remain with an activity appeared to include a 'permitting adult'. Here, an activity might be started either by the child itself, or by an adult who would settle the child down. That adult, or another, would then remain near the child, aware of what the child was doing but not interfering in it; available to respond if a response was requested, yet often doing something quite unrelated to the child's own activity; above all simply present. Two examples of this are the following, both recorded in Runnymede.

During the tissue collage already described, the adult left the table at the point where she was satisfied that the child had understood the technique of crumpling and sticking the paper. At that point the boy found himself alone at the table, He craned round immediately to see what other children in the room were doing. After a moment, he stuck a few pieces of tissue down himself. It was then that the new boy came to the table, producing the episode where the original child shifted the newcomer's tissue ball to the perimeter of the circle. Just then another adult arrived and sat down, saying to the newcomer, 'Shall I tell you how to do it? You take a bit like this (crumpling it between her fingers) dip it in the glue and pop it down there. That's right. You do it now.' When this second adult moved away as the first had done, the boy gazed after her for a moment before returning to his collage. He then became aware of the observer sitting about four feet away, and interested in what he was doing; possibly even writing down what he was doing. He no longer twisted round in his chair to look for the more familiar adults, but continued to work, glancing at her from time to time. If she caught his eye he would smile, hunching his shoulders slightly, sighing, and continuing with his work. The other child, who had made a scruffy and incomplete football compared with the one that the older boy was working on, said he had finished and received loud praise and encouragement from the adult who had started him on the collage. The boy looked at the other child's effort and back to his own – neater and more skilful, but still incomplete – and for a moment appeared tempted to stop. However, he looked back at the observer and then completed the circle, getting up finally to show it to the adult who started him off. 'Oh, that's very nice,' she exclaimed. 'That's very nicely done. Do you want to do it in the middle now?' (i.e. fill in the football). He shook his head, and she made no attempt to get him to change his mind. 'Do you want to do something else?' His gaze shifted past her to the large hall where children were running round and calling out, and she interpreted this: 'Do you want to go and play in the big room?' He nodded and went past her out to the big room.

On another occasion, some sustained and repetitive activity was seen with some bricks that interlocked with each other. The game of building towers and watching them fall continued as long as the adult sat at the table with the child, laughing at each renewed disaster. The adult took no part in the building, but her presence, and obvious enjoyment of his game appeared to make it more rewarding. Once she left the table, he completed the tower he had been building, broke it deliberately, shouting BANG as it fell; and got up and left the table.

For the majority of children perhaps, an adult woman is a reassuring figure; and it may merely be that, in the absence of a parent, a child needs to know that he is not abandoned or alone in order to feel it is safe to give his full attention to what he is doing. The boy described above turned round each time an adult left his table to see where she was going and what the other children were doing – possibly simply to reassure himself that they were still there. Only one nursery (Vienna Close) seemed to be aware that one could increase the likelihood of a child's remaining at an activity, either by removing distractions or by providing encouragement, however discreetly.

In this instance, a child had taken up a drawing he did earlier in order to continue with it.

> The adult, seeing a boy with a large sheet of paper spread out on the table on which he was drawing in an intent manner, enticed away another boy who looked as if he were going to interfere, offering to read him a story. The drawing boy was thus left alone in the area of the room in which he was working, looking up only occasionally when the two hamsters in the cage near him made a rattling noise.

> When the boy had finished his drawing he took it to the staff member saying excitedly 'Jane, look at this, look at this!' 'Oh yes!' she answered, 'you've drawn lots of cars on it now, you didn't have cars on it before.'

On another occasion, it was the presence of an adult at the table, and his comments on the children's activities that encouraged them to persist.

> 'OK, Susanna, you've chosen to play with the rods.' He sat at the table with three children and helped them remove the Cuisenaire rods from the box in order to have a pile each.

> 'Johnny, can I put some back?'

> 'See what you can do with these first of all. You might want some more, or you might want to put some back.'

> The three children played with the rods. A small pre-verbal child began to fit rods back in the box, unsuccessfully at first (each colour/length has its own section).

> 'No, not there, not that one – yes, that's right – good.'

> The older child wanted to do it too.

> 'Susanna, will you wait until Janine has finished?'

> A few moments later Susanna put the rest of her rods back in the box; a third child was still playing with the rods.

> 'That's very good. That's very clever! You've made a train going under a bridge. Would you like some animals for your train – shall I get some?'

Another nursery (Birkett) is worth mentioning individually because of the unusual number of children in it capable of focused and sustained activity. They were all of them the children of students, neither poverty-stricken nor from families with obvious problems, and it is tempting, although not particularly illuminating, to suppose that it was the nature of their home life that enable them to play for long periods on their own; in games such as Lotto for instance, involving a capacity to organize their behaviour around quite complicated rules. To the extent that children model their behaviour upon that of their adults, the parents appeared to have had some effect. The nursery itself made little attempt to capitalize upon their children's abilities, but, like Runnymede, employed the presence of the 'permitting adult' to good effect.

Grouping the children

The large group

At some point during every nursery's day there was a time when all the children, or all those within a unit, were brought together to engage in a single activity. In some nurseries this might be done for administrative convenience – at lunch for instance, or during an expedition to the park – but often it appeared to be done because group activities were seen to serve other ends as well. Frequently, large groups were created for story-reading, which of course had useful side effects for the staff which cannot be discounted; it freed all but one of them to get on with other activities, whether clearing up and preparing the tables for the midday meal, or having a cup of coffee in peace.

However, group-time for anything other than story-reading occurred with varying degrees of success. The following examples illustrate the extremes found in a nursery day.

In Wilberforce, the educational content of the day was felt to be very important.

> A lot of time was spent during circle-time in getting the children to sit quietly. Nothing, it appeared, was going to begin until the children were quiet, and there were a lot of warning cries

and admonitory noises: 'Just because I go out of the room, Gary Watkins, doesn't mean you can chatter. Shall we all sit down now? SHALL WE ALL SIT DOWN NOW – and I can do the register. WHEN YOU'RE ALL QUIET. Turn round, Trevor . . . Sit down, Jason, why do you have to ruin it? Now let's see who's going to sit the quietest, the boys or the girls.' The only time the teacher achieved the level of quietness she was after was when she called the register. However, they chatted freely when they were drinking their milk, which they collected one at a time from the teacher sitting at the head of the circle. During this period there were constant shouts for quietness from the teachers and general crossness ('You'll be sitting there to the end, young man!') none of which seemed to affect a fairly high level of noise, within which children got up and moved around, talked to each other, stamped their feet on the floor, banged their cups on the chairs, argued and cried. At one point, the staff member leading the group told a child to go to the kitchen to collect some Ribena. When another child jumped to go too, he was told to stay, but he ignored it and pushed his way out of the circle. Shouting, but helpless, the member of staff called out that the original child was to be allowed to carry the bottle back. The two boys left the room together, wrestling and punching each other; the fight continued in the kitchen, because the cook put her head through the hatch to ask who was supposed to be collecting the Ribena. The rightful owner eventually returned with the bottle, virtuous and triumphant, assaulted by his rival all the way back to the circle.

In another nursery, the nursery nurse organizing circle time eventually succeeded in achieving the silence she was after.

A small boy had volunteered to sing 'This Old Man'. He began with 'he played two,' but was corrected by the nursery nurse and told to start again with 'one'. He said 'give a dog a bone' indistinctly and was snapped at to do it again: 'You can talk properly, can't you?' When he had finished, the nursery nurse instructed the rest of the group not to clap because she didn't think he had done it at all well. Later, discouraged, this child was slow to 'wake up' during the final verse of 'Peter plays with one hammer'. He was shouted at by the nursery nurse: 'You know,

Stephen, you make me cross, because you're the eldest here, and I don't know why, you behave the stupidest.'

Events were very different within the all-day playgroup. Circle-time occupies an important place within the playgroup philosophy, and was an invariable part of the day's activity within this nursery.

At half past ten each morning, children were told to leave what they were doing and to take their chairs into the hall for drink-time. The chairs were then arranged by both children and adults in a semi-circle facing a table by which the adult sat. During the period when the children were settling down into the semi-circle, many went off to take a book each from the book corner and look quietly at it until everyone was ready for their drink. In spite of this expectation, during the ten minutes or so it took for everyone to be settled, the children chatted to each other, chanted, poked at their next door neighbours, wandered around till told to sit down, complained, hummed and laughed. Eventually they were told 'Shush! Listen very carefully as I call your name out or you might not hear your own name!' – whereupon the chattering died down to a whisper. The children came to the table one by one as their names were called and were given a small amount of either warm or cold milk, as they chose, which they drank when they were sitting down again. Each child, as it finished, got up and dropped its plastic cup into an empty washing-up bowl in the middle of the semi-circle and returned to its place. Eventually two of the older children were given the two china jugs to take back to the lady in the kitchen; yet another took the tray, and another the bowlful of empty cups. The two boys raced back together; 'Good boys!' They were followed more sedately by a small girl who said, 'I didn't run.' 'Good girl,' replied the adult, 'Musn't run!'

Milk was followed by songs. Four or five activity songs were sung, often involving number, or naming parts of the body, with vigorous participation especially for 'If you're happy and you know it, stamp your feet!' or 'March around!' The group songs were followed by several of the older children coming to the front and singing songs on their own. The end of each song, however hesitant or inaudible, was followed by generous applause. No child was encouraged to sing, but they didn't need to be: there were plenty of volunteers among the older children.

At the beginning of one group session, the adult in charge that morning capitalized on some quietly rebellious footstamping. 'Stand up everyone who's cold! Now come on, let's have some footstamping and some hand-clapping, so's we get warm again!' There was a terrific response to this, and when the children sat down again they were quiet.

Silence was only rarely attempted in a day nursery, and very rarely indeed achieved. It was noticeable that those nurseries which permitted a lot of noise at some part of the day had less difficulty in establishing quiet when it was necessary, for instance during a story, or at circle-time. Children also seemed more willing to be quiet in one room if there was another in which they might be noisy; here, of course, an outdoor play area is invaluable.

The side effects of large group activity such as that described in the playgroup are of course that children learn to wait; to take turns; to appreciate another's efforts, however clumsy; to empathize; to follow rules. Group activity involves, in fact, a fairly intense burst of socializing and social learning. In addition, a successful circle-time seemed to form a focus for the day, in which it was implicitly recognized that the nursery had a corporate identity, was a community with its own history and traditions independent of who was or was not present on that occasion.

Such sharing of experiences can make it more likely that the attitudes of the adults are conveyed and handed on to the children (a fact that is unfortunately as true of bad as of good practice). Each style of practice generates more of the same.

During an action song about a teddy bear, sung at circle-time, a new boy remained sitting down, uncertain of what he was supposed to be doing. An older boy who had been sitting beside him put his arm encouragingly around the smaller one's back, gesturing to him to join in with the rest of them. When the new boy shook his head, the other boy continued with his song unperturbed. The exchange was seen both by the staff member leading the song and the younger boy's mother; and they smiled at each other across the heads of the children while continuing to sing.

Small groups

Although the large group was used by some nurseries only for administrative rather than social reasons, every nursery divided into small groups from time to time, either formally or informally.

The membership of the *informal small group* was often selected by the children themselves, and might change over a period of time. Commonly, such a group might gather spontaneously at a table where an activity had already been laid out. In one kind of informal group the adult would start the children on an activity, but then leave them alone to structure the session themselves. There was a slight risk here that an assertive child might take control of the group himself.

> On three occasions, at one nursery, games of Pelmanism or Lotto were played by groups of children on their own, once the cards had been provided by a staff member. In one game of Lotto it became apparent during the free and animated chatter between the five children playing that there was actually considerable collusion between Jamie, the caller, and his friend Ralph. It was made explicit to the others when Ralph announced 'I'm the winner!' and Jamie answered, 'No, you're not, not yet; I'd better find your last card.' He rummaged around in the box until he came up with the card Ralph needed, whereupon the two of them left the game. The others did not protest, as older children would certainly have done, but after a moment's hesitation searched in the box themselves for the pictures they needed to complete their own cards.

In some nurseries *formal groups* were created, whose structure was determined by the adult: in Nightingale House and Marshall, children were divided into the under-threes and the over-threes, and the activities suited to the age group. Sometimes this was done for the express purpose of giving the older group 'lessons', a special case of small-group activity. Although there is certainly a case for separating the two-year olds from the rising-fives for at least part of the day, there seemed no reason why it should be a permanent arrangement.

In two nurseries the leadership of the various groups was deliberately rotated, in order that the staff should not become too specialized in dealing with one age group. This increased the instability of the setting for the child, since it meant that the adults as well as the children in each group changed quite frequently. In fact, because the private nurseries were smaller than the State nursery, there was less need to subdivide the children into groups; only Osborne Place and Nightingale House had more than 27 children. With one exception (Nightingale), age groupings were only used for a small part of the day. Osborne Place also used a rudimentary family grouping system, only operating at meal times.

Nurseries where control of the children was a major issue divided the children into small groups more often and for more of the time than did nurseries where the emphasis was on free play. In Wilberforce, a nursery in which control was a predominating theme, for half the morning the children were divided into four groups according to age and/or ability and each group allotted to an adult. This nursery expressed some ambivalence about grouping the children on an age/ability basis; the Organizer said that she knew ability grouping was not regarded favourably in educational circles, but that they found it 'worked best' for them. Here, the youngest group might spend its time playing in the wendy house, while the oldest engaged in a session with the 'feely' box.

> Each child was asked to choose something out of a box on the table (a shell, a coin, an empty cotton reel, a large button, etc.) and to find, through touch alone, the same object from among a jumble of other objects inside the 'feely' box. As the child fumbled for the matching object, the teacher conducted a conversation with the group about the nature of the object the child was looking for. One such object was a seashell: 'It's smooth, isn't it? Where do you find shells? Yes, at the seaside. Have you been to the seaside? With your Daddy?'

However, although the small group can afford the opportunity for a qualitatively different and valuable experience in which the participants may unite in pursuing a common goal, when the adult in charge has a very specific and clearly defined end in view, the very clarity of her intentions may inhibit the development of a harmonious and united group. On this occasion, a lighthearted attempt to weave a fantasy around some spilled paint was brought zealously back to earth.

'That's nice, Keith; careful not to put it on the floor. What's that?' (She points to paint on his hand.)

'That's bleeding!'

'Is that the right colour for bleeding? What colour is bleeding?' (Pause)

'It's blood, isn't it? What colour is blood?'

'Red.'

'Yes, red. And what colour has Keith got on his fingers?'

'Yellow.'

'Yes, yellow; so it's not bleeding, is it?'

The most productive small groups were a *third kind*, those in which, although *membership was determined by the children, an adult was available, although not necessarily participating*.

This time felt-tipped pens, and coloured paper already gummed on the back were available, rather than pictures. 'This paper's got glue on the back, it's meant to be for cutting up into shapes. Well, you don't have to, you can do whatever you like with it, but it's meant to be for sticking.' Seven children settled at the table to cut, lick and stick the paper with no more encouragement than the above comment from the member of staff. The children talked as they worked, occasionally about what their picture represented but more often about unrelated topics – birthday parties, or ferocious friends or who was the oldest present. The children worked independently in that none copied what another was doing – one boy drew a rocket, another next to him was interspersing cut-out squares with drawn circles. The staff member occasionally sat by the table, but got up too, and sometimes stood talking to her colleague about unrelated matters. The smallest boy present at the table held up his paper to the adult. It had several cut-outs stuck on it and a few hieroglyphs. The adult asked him where his name was, and he pointed to the hieroglyphs. She then wrote his name clearly on the paper for him and asked him to copy it. He refused, so instead she offered him further pieces of coloured paper. He added two more cut-outs to his picture, and then got up with the paper, walked across the room and added it to the pile of completed work without showing it again to the adult. He then went back to the table to watch the boy who was drawing a rocket.

This example could be duplicated many times from those nurseries that felt able to grant their children that degree of independence over how they employed the materials provided.

The under-twos

We have been writing as though life in a day nursery began at the age of two, or even older. For the majority of children this is true, but three of the nine nurseries we visited took a few children under the age of two, and all of them had long waiting lists. There was no reason to assume that any nursery capable of catering for under-twos would not have been full immediately. However, the demands, both physical and emotional, upon a nursery that undertakes the care of babies are considerable. In both the State nurseries catering for the under-twos, the babies were looked after in a separate room from the other children. The move from the babies' room into the general day nursery was a very gradual one, and the pace was set by the individual child. As soon as a toddler began to show interest in what the other children were doing he was encouraged to wander into the day nursery and spend short periods of time there. As the amount of time spent away from the babies' room increased, the decision was taken to attach the child to another family group. At Nightingale House (the only private nursery which took under-twos) the definition of babyhood was made not in terms of social adjustment, but of feeding schedules: as soon as a baby of nine months or so was ready to go on to solid foods three times a day it was moved out of the baby room.

Vienna Close saw the mother and infant as a unit, and encouraged them to attend together: the mother cared for her baby herself within the nursery as she might have done at home, but with the crucial difference that she was surrounded by sympathetic, helpful and experienced adults who could help her through the difficult patches. Although Vienna Close would care for a baby while its mother, for instance, went shopping, they felt their role to be quite as useful to the mother as to the infant. By example, support, and the sharing of experience, the mother was enabled to perceive her child as a potential

source of pleasure rather than as an intolerable burden. This feeling
was given expression when, finding no infants present for the second
time running, the chief staff member in this group said, laughing, that
at least they knew they must be doing a good job if no one turned up;
the mothers only came when they felt unable to cope with their babies
themselves.

> On a typical morning three babies and five adults, smoking and
> chatting and drinking coffee, were in the sitting room. The
> observer had one of the only two chairs and the others were sit-
> ting on the floor or on cushions. There was a marked tolerance
> for the inadequacy of two of the mothers present – one of whom
> was continuing to leaf through a mail-order catalogue while her
> infant girl who had fallen lay whimpering a few feet away from
> her. The staff tended for the infants in a gentle and unofficious
> manner – they offered a hand to a fallen toddler, a lap to a crying
> one or a share of a biscuit or piece of fruit to any child within
> reach. All such interaction, though, was mindful of the presence
> of the mother and was careful not to preempt her role of respon-
> sibility. The quality of conversation between the group leader and
> a mother made that mother seem more a friend than a client; they
> talked about buying things for her new flat, and how she was
> planning to decorate it; the price of paints and paint scrapers. 'I
> must come up and see it one day,' the group leader said with
> enthusiasm; and later that morning they left together with the
> baby, to go to Woolworths to buy brushes.

In marked contrast to this was the way the infants were cared for in
Nightingale House. This nursery seemed to find it difficult to share
responsibility with the mother.

> The three-month old infant was still being breast-fed, by a
> mother who came in at lunchtime to feed him. There seemed a
> tacit agreement on the part of the staff that this was a bad thing.
> At 11.10, less than an hour before he was due to be fed, one of
> the staff gave him a cupful of diluted orange juice, and then an-
> nounced to her colleague how hungry he had been. 'I don't think
> she gives him enough.' This was capped by another staff member
> saying, 'Well, yesterday she said she didn't think he'd taken

enough. So perhaps it'd be a good idea to give him the bottle at lunchtime. Mmm. Well, see how it goes.' At 11.25 a nurse picked up this infant and announced to it 'I don't think your mother gives you enough! I think I'm going to feed you.'

The chances were, for that day at least, that it would not go well: a baby full of orange juice and cereal will not take much breast milk. From this nursery's point of view, therefore, there was no room for both mother and staff member to care for the same child. The mother's ambivalence about her decision to let the nursery care for her child was shown in her attempt to reserve for herself a central feature of the mother-infant relationship – feeding – and the nursery nurses' feeling that the mother was not behaving appropriately was expressed in their unconscious attempts to sabotage the lunch-time feed. Within this nursery, the sharing of care was not possible: the mother was being obliged to choose between taking the baby away altogether, or letting the nursery assume the sole responsibility for the daily feeding schedule.

The third nursery caring for under-twos, Paul Street, neither rejected the parents nor made a special point of including them. The staff in this room had had children of their own, and treated their charges with brisk affection, if a certain lack of intimacy. If parents wanted to stay they were accepted with a complete lack of ceremony, but the responsibility for the baby was seen by both parent and staff to be the nursery's.

Neither this nursery, therefore, nor Nightingale House appeared able to face sharing responsibility for the child. It is an issue at all ages and stages of day-care of course, but one that is particularly critical with the infants. By acknowledging it as an issue, Vienna Close was able to evolve a constructive policy towards sharing responsibility. No member of staff there showed any tendency to 'poach' a baby, as we have described in Nightingale House.

We return at this point to the question asked at the beginning of the chapter: what is life in the day nursery like for the child? Our descriptions of the styles of organization and experiences available to the child cannot of course provide an answer, but inevitably the reader must have begun to respond to the episodes described, sometimes with warmth, sometimes with dismay; to have begun to form some picture of the kind of nursery to which he might contemplate sending a child of his own. Yet a comparison of circle-time at Runnymede with the same activity at Wilberforce makes it clear that within broad limits it is not so much *what* is done as *how* it is done that is determining the nature of that response. Thus in the next chapter, we shall take a closer look at the factors responsible for the *how*, rather than the *what* of nursery life.

5

Adults and children face to face

The major determinant of the nature of the child's experience in the day nursery has been touched upon in the preceding chapter without ever being specified. It is perhaps the most difficult feature of day nursery life to comprehend with any degree of objectivity and yet it is also critically important.

Time and time again during these observations we found that one of the most basic factors determining the quality of life for a particular child in a particular nursery was the kind of relationship that existed between the adults and the children. There seemed to be a real distinction between those nurseries that had achieved a means of ensuring a mutually satisfying and rewarding day for both adult and child, and those for whom each day involved the constant threat of conflict and chaos.

Fundamental to this distinction were diverging views about the purposes of day care institutions. For instance, individual nurseries, and indeed individual members of staff, varied considerably in the amount and degree to which they could bring themselves to allow the children to get on with their own day. At one of the nurseries we visited (Birkett) we commented that the children were sometimes left for quite long periods of time unsupervised in the television room or the corridor. The Organizer replied that she was always 'listening out', and in fact they did not get many fights or squabbles. 'If they fall over, well they fall over. *We let them get on with whatever they want to do.*' (Our italics.) Here, the day nursery was believed to exist for the child to use as it felt best, with adult assistance when necessary.

This philosophy contrasted strongly with that of Wilberforce, where the staff always knew exactly what was going to happen at a particular time of day, and wanted the children to 'sit quietly in a space with arms folded' while waiting for a new activity to begin. Their assumption was that it was the adults who knew best: they had the major, if not sole, responsibility for the way in which the day was to be spent.

These divergent views about the purposes of day-care institutions were usually fairly explicit, with nurseries falling into one category or the other. Closely correlated with these two views were the nurseries' differing opinions about the inherent nature of the young child; although considerably less explicit, they were quite as influential a factor in determining staff behaviour.

One view saw children as basically responsible and capable of self-direction towards appropriate ends; they were accordingly encouraged to choose their own activities, participate in group decisions ('shall we take our lunch outside and have it on the grass or shall we go outside afterwards?') and help with the running of the community. Children at Runnymede or Vienna Close, for example, were expected to pick up the toys, carry the cups to the kitchen without dropping them, or help a younger child to find a place at circle time. The adults behaved to the children as though they believed the children shared their own aims and intentions and had roughly the same expectations of the day. Buried within this approach was the implicit assumption that the most effective controls of behaviour were those that stemmed from the child rather than from the adult. The expectation in this setting, therefore, was the adults would foster and make use of the child's own developing internal controls; the adult's role could be seen as primarily that of a model, rather than a policeman. Where, by and large, this state of affairs existed in a nursery, we refer to it as a *positive alliance*.

The other view of young children saw them as fundamentally un-directed and unruly, and hence incapable of sustained or sensible activity without adult supervision. Controls of behaviour here were accordingly imposed externally, rather than nurtured within the children themselves. No positive alliance can exist where the adults have at the back of their minds the fear or even the conviction that the children will not want to hear the story, will prefer to throw their food around rather than eat it, draw on the books rather than read them and fight their neighbours rather than play with them. And as so often happens, the belief greatly increases the chances of the prophecy's being fulfilled, and creates a vicious circle. An alliance exists all right, but it is *negative*, producing increasingly troubled relations between adult and child.

The underlying causes of these staff-child relationships are explored more fully in the final chapter, but for the moment here are some examples of such alliances, positive and negative, or successful and un-successful, in action.

The existence of these positive or negative 'sets' in relationships between adult and child is seen in, amongst other things, the way they speak to one another. In this nursery, a staff member was looking at some drawings on a piece of paper held by a child.

> 'Is that yours, Dean? Did you do that? Can I see it, will you show it to me? Did you do those?'
>
> 'Tracey did them – she did them for me,' replied the child innocently.
>
> The teacher reacted as though she had detected a major art forgery.
>
> 'Well, I'm not going to put *your* name on it if Tracey did it!'
>
> The child took the drawing away silently, folding it up very small and stuffing it into his pocket. The teacher turned to a colleague and said, affronted, '*She* did it for him – I saw her do it with a pencil.'

Misunderstandings of course can occur at any time; the point of this episode was that it stemmed directly from the adult's assumption that the child was attempting to deceive her. That having his name on a drawing might mean for him ownership rather than authorship was not part of that particular adult's view of the nature of children. Moreover, the adult had revealed by the end of the exchange that she had already known that the drawing was not Dean's work; her original question was intended to catch him out.

Similarly in Osborne Place the tone of voice of the staff suggested that they expected trouble from the start.

> It is possible to deliver a statement such as 'Go inside and take off your overall' in a number of ways, ranging from warm, through neutral and along a scale of control and command until it is an irritated shout. Statements to the children in this nursery by all but one member of staff were invariably delivered in a tone of voice well beyond the neutral and towards the irritable. Contained within the manner of delivery was the implication that the child might well not do what it has been asked to do, and thus a certain amount of pre-emptive irritation was appropriate, indeed necessary.

By way of contrast, in another nursery (Runnymede), there was a great deal more conversation from the start, both between the children themselves and between staff and children. The significance of these dialogues lay in the fact that it was impossible to tell from the tone of voice alone (the content, of course, might differ) whether an adult was addressing a child or another adult. There was no signalling to the child by the manner in which it was addressed that here was an adult who expected defiance, and was determined to nip all trouble in the bud. Conversation was conducted between equals, with modifications for lack of experience taking place in the content, rather than the style. Here, for example, a group of children in the smaller room were playing with lumps of clay. An adult (the playleader for that day) was at the table with them:

> 'I'm going to make a fish, a sausage-fish.'
>
> '*I've* got a birthday cake.' Two clay-modelling tools were stuck in it for candles. The cake then got flattened out with a fist, and a face was drawn on it.
>
> 'Where's his teeth then, has he got any teeth?' asked an adult.
>
> 'My Dad's got a beard like *that*,' a child said, gesturing with fingers to his upper lip.
>
> 'Has he got any there?' asked the adult, pointing to the clay-man's chin.
>
> 'No.'
>
> 'Then it's a moustache. You know, a moustache.'
>
> 'Like Steve Austin?'
>
> 'Yeah,' said the adult.
>
> 'My Dad's got a moustache like Steve Austin!'
>
> 'I saw you on Steve Austin last night,' said another child to the adult. 'You were Jamie.'
>
> She laughed and told another adult, 'He thinks I was Jamie on Steve Austin last night!'
>
> 'I had a birthday yesterday.'
>
> 'You told me that last week,' said the adult. 'Who had it yesterday then?'
>
> 'I had one last week too!'

This unselfconscious participation in a general conversation was typical of the young staff in this group, many of whom had children of

preschool age of their own. It was noticeable in this nursery how often
an adult would be amused or pleased at something a child had done or
said, and would repeat it, laughing, to a colleague. The capacity to
enjoy the childishness of children, rather than to fear or dislike it, may
be at the very least desirable for parenthood, but it is crucial for a good
caretaking relationship.

The existence of a positive or negative alliance is demonstrated of
course in many ways, of which the manner of staff-child dialogue is
one of the more obvious. Other important areas in which it can be seen are
in the nature of the staff's non-verbal relationships with the children: for
example, the way in which they comfort or reassure a distressed child; the
way in which they achieve control, and their attitude to discipline; and the
ways in which they encourage or make possible the development of
autonomy in the children.

We discuss these areas in more detail in the following sections.

Language

Both the style and the content of language were important factors in
adult-child relationships. The most critical feature of language in day
nurseries is of course that there should be some; and there were many
nurseries in which very little conversation at all took place – between
adults, between children, and in particular between adults and children,
or children and adults.

Osborne Place, as has already been indicated, was uniquely lacking
in this respect. The ostensible reason given for the children's not being
allowed to speak to each other in their own language was that if they
did they would not learn to speak English. Yet in order for them to
learn English they surely ought to have been exposed to it, bathed in it,
whereas in fact time and time again opportunities for learning,
struggles to find the right word, were passed up by the adults in favour
of an orderly progression to the day. For instance a member of staff
held up a picture of the giant while reading Jack and the Beanstalk.
One or two children said, 'He's a nice giant!' which was countered by
other children saying 'No he's not, he's nasty!' The teacher's reaction
was to say at once, 'Now don't let's argue about it,' and the conversation ended.

Another example of a missed opportunity for language development has already been given on page 53, where a chance to engage in a conversation that was clearly of great significance for the child was passed up in favour of the rote repetition of a sentence about the date and weather. (Also unusual in this nursery was the number of children who approached the observer, eager to engage in conversation about themselves, their families and their homes, and difficult to reject.)

An inevitable result of the ban upon Punjabi in this nursery was that it enormously increased the staff's control over the children. Marshall, Nightingale and on occasions Wilberforce also used silence as a means of control, with, as has been described, limited success.

Other nurseries, for quite different reasons, had few extended conversations between their members. Sometimes this happened in a nursery where there was instead much non-verbal contact and communication. In Paul Street for instance, it was common, almost habitual, for an adult passing a child to ruffle its hair saying, 'Hello, Gary. All right? Hello, Tracy. All right?' It was a greeting that did not seem to expect an answer, but was given and received merely as a token of affectionate concern. On the other hand, in this same nursery, opportunities for language that a nursery with more specifically educational aims would have seized upon were missed altogether. During a game of Animal lotto, a child asked 'What are those sticks? I got one with the sticks!' – to be told simply, 'They're not sticks, they're horns – the antelope's horns.'

The presence of language alone, however, could not guarantee a positive alliance. Dough-making in Wilberforce, for example, (page 49) produced a stream of clear, explicit instructional language from the adult in charge, but almost nothing from the children engaged equally in the task. There were three nurseries that used language more fully or in ways that were not only to do with information or instruction. Birkett children, perhaps because the children came from unusually (in terms of day-nursery populations) articulate parents, talked a great deal among themselves, using language about themselves, their feelings and impressions, their inner preoccupations. Runnymede produced a lot of amiable chatter both between children and between adults and children, of which the example quoted on page 72 is characteristic. The content of such conversations is in some ways irrelevant, forming as they do the small change of communication;

what is conveyed to the child by the adult's participation is a friendly interest in his life both inside and outside the nursery.

Vienna Close was once again the nursery that stood out in its constant and varied use of language between and across all levels, children, organizers, volunteers, kitchen staff and parents.

This example occurred during the reading to three children of a story about a visit to the seaside; the picture was of a crab.

> 'Yes, it's a crab! Do you remember how they walk? Sideways! Yes, sideways! I don't know any other animal that walks sideways! And what are these? Pincers! For picking bits of food up and putting it in their mouths. Because they eat other animals. Most animals eat other animals. You can eat crabs. I don't like them, but I like eating prawns and shrimps. They go pink when they're cooked. You pull their heads and tails off and then . . . num-num!'

The richness of the information offered may well be more than a four-year-old can digest, delivered at that speed, but the interest and enthusiasm manifested in the book through such a commentary was infectious. When the story ended there was a brief tussle over which of the three children who had been listening was going to keep the book to look at the pictures.

In another group, a large motherly woman who used to be one of the cleaners was sitting with a small boy on her lap; he was in the process of making the transition from the infants to an older children's group. They were sitting by the sandpit.

> 'Can you do that?' She held up her hand with the fingers spread widely. 'Look, one, two, three, four, five fingers you've got. Can you use them to put the sand in the bucket? . . . Like this, pick it up, now turn it upside down and what have you got, Anil? Ooooh, look, a sandcastle, a lovely sandcastle; . . . now you do it, Anil, Anil do it, pick it up and do it. . . .' Anil remarked, 'It's a pudding.' 'What kind of pudding is it? . . . Is it an apple pudding or is it an orange pudding?' 'It's a lovely apple pudding . . . num num num . . . no, I've had enough thank you, it was a lovely pudding, oh it *was* lovely, but it's all gone now . . . Oh, no Anil, leave it in the container, don't tip it out all over the floor and all over you

. . . *and* all over me.' Anil stayed on her lap while she continued to sit by the sand tray. A moment later another child brought plastic farm and zoo animals over to the sand, and the conversation turned to animals.

In this episode, the activity had been selected by the child; the adult took the initiative in making sandcastles, but was instantly willing to relinquish it as the child took the lead again and transformed the castle into a pudding. They shared that game for a while until the adult set limits to the activity by pointing out the area where it was permitted to use the sand. Instruction, direction, expressions of pleasure and imagination, all occurred in less than two minutes. There was no other nursery we visited that matched Vienna Close for the quantity and quality of its conversation.

We include a final example in order to give a glimpse of the variety of the ways in which this nursery used language. The conversion of a moment's conversation between the two adults into a game which everyone could play was charmingly and spontaneously achieved.

A boat trip was planned for the afternoon. The group leader suggested that she, with three of the older children go out for a walk that morning, down to the shops, because they were going to have to sit still all afternoon. A general clear-up was necessary before they went; she asked a child to put the record up on the shelf, telling him they'd play it later when they came back from buying food. A moment later her assistant entered the room, and the group leader said, incorporating the children who were to accompany her with a gesture like a conductor, 'Maggie, we're going out, down to the ———, to buy some ———, ('For *all* the kids!' interjected a child) 'to take on the ——— this afternoon.' The children who were to accompany her filled in the missing words in a chorus, grinning.

Contact and comfort

The amount of physical contact between adults and children varied considerably between nurseries. The three nurseries catering for under-twos were special cases. Here there was an obligation on the part of the staff to respond to an infant as a substitute mother, which inevitably involved a lot of physical contact, whether for business or pleasure. The nurseries that catered from two-plus to five-year-olds, however, did not cuddle or touch the children as a matter of course, but more as an expression of the staff's individual tastes and attitudes. For some, it was clearly a pleasure to be able to take a child onto their lap for a cuddle (Vienna Close), or to pat the top of a head in passing (Paul Street).

To others, the idea that a child might appreciate a cuddle seemed never to have occurred. Nightingale House was remarkable in this respect, since it was one of the few nurseries to include very young babies. Twice, faced with an infant working itself up into an hysterical state, two separate members of staff bent over the respective playpens clucking and waggling a soft toy within a few inches of the infant's face, making it cry even harder. Both these babies were under one year old.

The Matron of this nursery at least would have liked to have the infants in a group of their own as she recognized that their needs and routines were different from those of the older children. However, although the Matron may have been aware that an infant may cry for simple contact, the other staff – possibly through pressure of time – were unwilling to carry a crying baby. They regarded a dirty nappy as the prime cause of distress. If a baby cried it provoked an immediate discussion among the staff present about how long it was since it had been changed, and whether it could possibly be 'dirty' again already. During a morning spent in the under-threes' room, there were three separate animated conversations among the staff present about someone 'smelling' in the room; the younger children were asked 'Are you dirty?' and each infant was sniffed at separately until the offender was found and borne off to be changed. If it wasn't 'dirty' or it wasn't near a meal-time, and could therefore be supposed to be hungry, it was assumed the infant was 'tired'. This meant that it was removed from the group and put to cry in a cot in a separate room. Since after a long period of crying the infant almost invariably did go to sleep, the diagnosis was seen as correct.

In this nursery, even allowing for the pressure of time and possible under-staffing, there seemed to be a real reluctance to cuddle the children. The actual cause of a child's distress – often separation from its mother – was vigorously ignored by the staff in favour of hunger, tiredness or minor ailments. ('He's got a rotten cold,' or 'It's his back teeth hurting him.') It was difficult to see why this should have been so. It may be that in a hospital setting, where the preoccupations are with physical illness and physical care, the emphasis of the nursery too had swung away from the consideration of emotional needs towards a less demanding role for the staff; moreover one that meshed satisfactorily with the preoccupations of the larger organization.

Nurseries with explicitly educational policies (Wilberforce, Marshall and Osborne Place) showed little physical contact with the children in keeping with their view of themselves as teaching, rather than caring for the children. In Wilberforce, a crying child was consoled indirectly by having the aggressor reprimanded. In Osborne Place, however, a child crying because it was her first morning at the nursery was carried by the Matron; but here mothers were explicitly discouraged from remaining with a child when it started at the nursery.

> In Marshall Nursery, the girl in charge of the children said angrily to a small boy who had told the observer that his mother was coming to collect him soon, 'Your mother is *not* coming, Tony, I've told you that before.' To a child who asked for her comforter, she said 'You don't *need* your flannel!' and then threw the comforter at the child so that it hit her on the chest before dropping to the floor: 'Well, take it anyway.' To a two-year-old who was attempting to show her the picture on the cover of a book, she said 'Choo-choo train – I *know*. You've already told me about sixteen times.'

Behaviour as distressing as this may not be common, and this girl had had no training for the job. However the potential effect of incidents like this upon the child is not mitigated by the knowledge that the adult is untrained.

A second group of nurseries also showed little physical contact with the children. Birkett and Runnymede both had an explicit policy of encouraging the mother to remain with the child until it was securely settled into the nursery. Moreover, neither of these nurseries catered for children who were from particularly deprived backgrounds: the majority of children had been at home with their mothers until they were two-and-a-half and had made the transition from home to nursery relatively uneventfully.

In Runnymede, a crying child would be comforted, although not necessarily cuddled. In Birkett, although there was little physical contact during the day, there was some particularly sensitive handling of the delicate transition period between a child's arrival at the nursery in the morning and its mother's departure.

> Both parents brought in a small half-Chinese boy. His mother was cuddling him, and he looked solemn and anxious; he did not want to leave her lap. The staff member came over and addressed him directly, touching his nose with her finger as she squatted down. 'Did you sleep last night, eh? Did you sleep?' The mother answered ruefully that no, he hadn't slept, and the staff member laughed. 'What have you brought today in your little bag?' she asked him. The child opened his cloth bag and showed her the contents, sliding off his mother's lap as he did so. The mother stood up, and placing her hand on the boy's back, the fingers extended so that only the tips were touching him, gave him the very gentlest of pushes, barely perceptible – although its message was clear. As she completed this gesture, the staff member took the child onto her own lap; and the mother left, waving. The child watched her go, expressionless, and then turned back to the staff member who continued to sit still, holding him, and asking him about the toys in his bag. She asked him twice if he'd like to take his coat off; the second time he agreed, and got up to go outside to hang it up. When he returned, the staff member was exactly where he had left her; but after glancing at her he joined a group of children.

This adult's behaviour had, in an unrushed and unobtrusive manner, allowed the initiative in that situation to pass from the mother to her, and through her to the child. Only when she had seen that he was ready to take control of his own behaviour did she turn to other affairs.

The three remaining nurseries (Paul Street, Church Road, Vienna Close), all of them State nurseries, showed the highest incidence of physical contact between staff and children. At Paul Street adults ruffled hair, patted cheeks; at Church Road in one group's room there was the same constant and casual contact with the children – an arm round a child who was being encouraged to eat, a hug for the first child to be out in musical chairs. However, although crying children at both these nurseries received immediate comfort and attention, anxious and withdrawn children could be overlooked, particularly out of doors. At Paul Street:

> On one hot day, a young girl who arrived late cried as her mother left, and was taken onto the lap of the student in the group (who on that occasion was the only member of staff available for that group). After a few minutes, when the child had stopped crying, the student put her panda into a toy pushchair and sent her outside with it. The child stood still and silently in the middle of the playground for the next twenty minutes, while the play of other children eddied round her. Whenever a child approached her, usually wanting to play with the pushchair themselves, she tightened her grip on it and the expression on her face changed from one of apprehension to one of acute anxiety and incipient tears. Twice during that period the tears welled over as a particularly determined boy tugged at the pushchair. The student stopped the boy from claiming the pushchair, but interpreted the small girl's distress as arising from that incident alone.

At Vienna Close, physical contact and comfort formed a vital part of the adult-child relationship. All staff carried children, cuddled them or took them on their laps, both when the children were distressed and seemed to need it, and when an adult seemed to feel like it. This nursery appeared to be the only one where the staff did not feel they had to be seen to be busy in order to be confident that they were doing their job. Their ability to be still as well as to clear up, organize or instruct, was unique among the nurseries we visited. On one occasion a group leader picked up a crying child and took it onto his lap, where for the next 15 minutes he sat quietly in a large chair with her, occasionally stroking her face, while chatting to the other children in the room. His stillness communicated itself to the other children, who played quiet games – looking at books, cutting out pictures from magazines.

It should not be forgotten that many of the staff in this nursery were concurrently training as child psychotherapists. No doubt they were attracted to that work in the first place because of an interest in and a liking for children, but their training also makes much of the importance of parent-child relationships. The implication is that it may well be possible for adults to learn to respond in a way that might, at first glance, be considered purely intuitive.

Discipline and control

As we indicated at the beginning of this chapter, lying at the heart of the positive alliance, since it is both cause and effect of its existence, is the way in which staff achieve control of the children. As has already become apparent, overt control of the children plays a much larger part in some nurseries' days than in others. What was interesting about the issue of control was not the end-product required by the different nurseries (clean hands, no fighting, children who say please and thank you, children who clear up their own toys, children who are silent for story-reading or circle-time) which did not differ fundamentally between nurseries. What did differ was the way that they attempted to achieve these ends; whether external controls were imposed upon the children from without, or internal controls were felt to be capable of operating from within the group.

Aggression between the children themselves was an issue that brought staff attitudes to discipline to the fore, The most common cause of a fight between children was a dispute over property, where it is often impossible for even the most scrupulously fair of adults to be sure of the rights and wrongs of the case. Some nurseries, however, were not interested in being 'fair', merely in preventing disputes. A clear example of external controls being preferred to internal occurred in Osborne Place where the Matron said that neither she nor her staff allowed children to argue, 'otherwise someone might get hurt'. Three minor disputes over property ended immediately by an adult's deciding who was to have the toy, or continue with the activity, and adult decisions were never challenged although they may have provoked some resentment.

The fact that this nursery did not allow its children, the majority of whom were non-English speaking, to address each other in anything other than English must have served to reduce the amount of overt dispute, although it by no means reduced tension over property.

In Wilberforce, there were frequent squabbles and tears. Tears often resulted from a child's not wanting to do something an adult was trying to make it do, like wash its hands. The staff did not intervene physically in disputes, but called or shouted to the children to stop what they were doing. At Nightingale House, staff were overtly critical of children who fought, not merely of the behaviour itself (as in Wilberforce) but of the characters of the children.

> The behaviour of a very small two-year old girl was commented upon loudly from the other side of the room by a staff member: 'You're getting a very naughty, spiteful little girl, now you just leave the others alone. (To the other staff:) You have to watch her, don't you!'

The further division of style in the adults' handling of aggression came between those who overtly condemned such behaviour as 'bad', or 'naughty', and those who merely tried to end the trouble. An example of the latter came from the Deputy Matron at Marshall, who, it should be noted, was off-duty at the time. She was making herself some coffee in the kitchen when she noticed through the window some tearful argument among the unsupervised children playing out-of-doors. No child was rebuked but the adult pointed out that if fights kept occurring over pieces of equipment, she would have to take them out of circulation altogether.

The approach to aggression that relied most heavily on internal controls occurred in the nurseries where the expression of hostility seemed least inhibited. It rebuked neither child nor behaviour, but indicated that different behaviour, or even the same behaviour in a different place, if that was what the children wanted, might be more profitable.

In Birkett, some persistent rough-and-tumble play from the older boys began to escalate in intensity and the staff member reacted by saying firmly,

> 'Listen, you can fight in the park if you like, but not in here; it's too *noisy*!'
> 'But we'll get dirty in the park.' (It had been raining.)
> 'Well that's too bad, isn't it.'

This approach did not mean that the adult could not eventually intervene when internal controls were inadequate.

In Runnymede, prolonged tussling made an adult take the contestants by the hands and lead them off suggesting they all 'go and be busy, shall we?'

In Vienna Close, two boys wrestled, shouting at each other, over the possession of a spade. They were watched, but not stopped by a male group leader who eventually remarked 'I thought you two were supposed to be friends.' A moment later he put his hand on the head of the boy trying to take the spade and told him to wait his turn.

In summary, attitudes on the part of the staff to aggression in the children (whether hostile or playful) were consistent with their attitude to any other activity. Those nurseries that felt confident enough of the children to permit them to express a certain amount of aggression also gave them enough time to attempt to resolve disputes themselves. Those nurseries, in contrast, that attempted to control the children's play also attempted to prevent the physical and even verbal expression of their inevitable conflicts.

Apart from aggression between the children, to which all nurseries responded in one way or another, different nurseries expended differing amounts of time and energy in attempting to get the children to do what they wanted. As we have described, some began by structuring the day in such a way that there was little leeway for child-initiated activity. However, getting the horse to drink remained the problem: it is one thing to have circle-time scheduled for 10.50 and another to see it carried out. Other nurseries had far less structure to the day. However in either case it was noticeable that the amount of visible effort expended in trying to keep order was not necessarily reflected in the amount of order achieved. We saw two basic approaches to control, which we have called the *confronting style* and the *cooperative style*.

A *confronting* style is, as its name implies, one that employs predominantly external controls, presenting the child with a direct instruction or command, either positive or negative; come over here, be quiet, get down, sit down, clear up, don't fight. A clear example of this style in action has already been quoted in the section on the Large Group (page 59).

In Nightingale House, the same technique was employed.

> 'All sitting up nicely, fold your arms. Do as I say or I'll put you in the corner; I'll smack you if you go on like that.' And 'Who was the last to use this pipe? Was that you, Simon? Did you chew the end? Well then, who did?' 'Jane.' 'Jane did you chew this pipe?' 'No.' 'Well, that's not what it's for is it? You're not supposed to chew it. Just wait till Mrs Beecham sees this.'

In these exchanges, the adult demonstrated what we have called a negative alliance in her lack of confidence in the children's ability to cooperate, even by telling the truth. She ignored in the second instance the child's denial of the crime and threatened her with a superior authority. The technique was to demand obedience, and to offer immediate retribution if it was not forthcoming: I'll put you in the corner, smack you, tell my boss about you.

What were the actual consequences of failure to conform? We saw no child smacked (although several were pushed into the desired position), saw no one stood in the corner, no one sent outside (although in Osborne Place a child was made to turn its chair away from the table).

And in fact, of course, the staff do not really intend to carry out the worst of their threats. It is this that ultimately demonstrates the ineffectiveness of the confronting style. Unless staff are prepared to go beyond the bounds of normal behaviour, there is absolutely nothing they can do if the children do not cooperate: at least one child will be whispering or wriggling, or pinching his neighbour to make *him* wriggle, when an adult is trying to quell a large group by direct confrontation. The consequence is that endless attempts to gain obedience take up much of the time, as they did during large group-time at Wilberforce. Moreover they create a disagreeable and tense atmosphere.

It is not possible to say whether, or how, the children were permanently affected by such behaviour. Perhaps little happened other than the steadily diminishing expectation of cooperation from both sides. However, that diminishing expectation was in fact the crux of the issue of control. Ultimately it is impossible to maintain control of a group of children without either using real punishment or, and it is a big 'or', gaining their cooperation; in effect, using them as the source of effective controls.

However, not every adult with a confronting style is either as un-successful, or as ill-disposed to the children as these examples might suggest. At Birkett, a brisk young woman with a cheerfully confident manner employed a confronting style to better effect than most others; for example when some children climbed onto the back of a forbidden sofa.

> 'Jamie! Just be careful,' the staff member called; and after a moment, when that had had no effect, 'Listen! Just let me tell you,' as she came over to them; 'If you climb on the back of there it does just what it did with Esther and it tips right over. So don't climb on there, right!' When the game continued without more than a moment's pause she followed it with a threat of enforced inactivity unless she was obeyed, and the boys ran off into the other room.

We suggest two reasons why her approach achieved a moderate amount of success. The first was that she was asking the children to stop doing something for a clearly stated reason: the sofa might tip and the children hurt themselves. It is a reason a child can follow and ap-preciate; a good reason in fact. The second was that in other respects and at other times her behaviour was helpful and companionable. There are inevitably moments in the best-run homes and nurseries when the stage of direct confrontation is reached!

The *cooperative* style of attaining order is as oblique as the confron-ting style is direct. Perhaps the clearest example is the one already quoted; the conversation of some rebellious foot-stamping during the large group at Runnymede into a united and constructive 'warming-up' session. At the same nursery we noticed an incident in which an adult distracted a child by asking him to name animal figures she was holding up in order to turn his attention away from a noisy game he'd been playing.

Many incidental remarks were heard: 'These bricks are so heavy I can't manage them on my own'. 'Joe is making such a noise I can't hear what Freddy wants,' (both Vienna Close). The technique involves offering the child a number of options, amongst which are help with the bricks, or less noise. It permits the desired result to emerge from the child's decision, rather than his submission, and hence appeals to his own internal sources of control.

And in fact, the choice is available to both the child *and* the adult: if the child does not cooperate, the adult also has a number of alternatives before being reduced to the direct confrontation: 'Do as I say, or else. . . .'

However successful a recipe this may be in theory, it cannot of course be employed out of context with the hope of success. The context to a large extent sets limits to the kinds of staff behaviour that are possible – that are neither unacceptable to the other staff nor incomprehensible to the children. 'Permitting' behaviour (see p. 55) within a nursery that operates a negative alliance can be resented by the other staff and misinterpreted by the children. Where external controls are habitually employed, whether successfully or not, it would be risky to rely upon internal controls during, for instance, a first attempt at spatter painting. The child all too easily comes to rely upon the adult, and the institution, for the means of controlling its impulses.

Thus the prevailing style within a nursery will tend to produce conformity whatever the newcomer's original inclinations; and the successful use of a cooperative style of control is therefore as much a symptom of a positive alliance as it is a cause.

Independence and autonomy

Every nursery we saw felt itself to be working towards the development of independence in the children. Yet, as usual, this meant different things to different nurseries, and was equally clearly related to the fundamental attitudes of the adults towards the children in their care. It was rare to find a nursery in which the children themselves were regarded as playing a significant part in the development of their nursery community; far more often, the organizers seemed to feel that only adults could initiate and communicate ideas. Runnymede was one of the few places which seemed to have capitalized on children's capacity to help one another. The introduction of a new child was used as an opportunity for giving responsibility to the older children. The bigger ones were encouraged to look after the little children, particularly if they went out for a walk or needed help in going to the lavatory.

The incident already described (on page 61), in which an older child encouraged a newcomer to take part in circle-time perhaps testifies to the success of this strategy. It was remarkable how few places there were in which children were reasonably free to choose what they did compared with the number of places in which their day was highly organized.

Every nursery, however, liked its children to learn to take care of themselves physically. For instance, all nurseries encouraged children to take themselves to the lavatory and wash their hands, and encouraged children to put on and take off their own outer garments. All nurseries also expected, or permitted, help with minor tasks, such as taking the cups to the kitchen after milk-time, or bearing a message from one section of the nursery to another.

Yet these standard measures of independence represent a very limited notion of what independence could mean. In a sense, it is the adult's rather than the child's independence that they provide; the adult is freed from the child's need for her to wash its hands, feed it lunch and button it into its coat. Often the adults who were most diligent in getting a child to achieve this kind of physical independence reacted with dismay to a search for a different kind of independence: that involving choice, decision, and eventually autonomy.

Even more than being able to take onself to the lavatory, the freedom to choose not only what or whom one will play with, and (within obvious limits) how one will play with one's toy or companion, could be what the child perceives as independence. Routes towards this goal must inevitably involve exploration, and the discovery of one's own as well as the adult's limits. It might be assumed that such exploration was one of the purposes of play; that through play with materials and play with companions and play on one's own, such discoveries could be achieved in a safe and enjoyable manner. Yet many nurseries actively prevented the development of knowledge through exploration, by determining not only what a child was permitted to play with, but also the way in which it was permitted to play. Finger-painting in Osborne Place, play with nesting cups in Church Road, or clay modelling in Marshall Day Nursery: each experience was limited for the child by the adult's view that there was a 'right' way to do these things; and imposing this view upon the child circumscribed its experience almost before it had begun. There were some toys, moreover, that in their basic design achieved the same end without the adult's ever having to lift a finger: colouring books, or fuzzy-felt pictures, even television. All these may have their place at times of the day, when a child wants to be occupied or entertained without exploring, to be passive, to retreat to safe ground. Yet we became wary of nurseries that had too many toys of this kind in evidence. We felt they were places where the adults employed toys to structure and limit the child's experience on their behalf.

We would not want to put forward a romantic's view of the inherent value of finger-painting. Yet the kind of independence that Vienna Close, for example, tacitly acknowledged to be important for both children *and* adults certainly involved the entire nursery in fewer restrictions on noise or mess during playtime; greater risk-taking, both physical and emotional; greater involvement of the staff in the children's lives both in and out of the nursery. It undoubtedly made greater demands upon the adults' time, energy and maturity than the staff of most nurseries could, or would want to meet. Yet it was also the nursery where cooperation between its members, large and small, was most in evidence and where the kind of independence we have suggested is most valuable visibly flourished.

In conclusion, it would be over-optimistic to suppose that free play with a wide choice of materials is on its own sufficient to enable a child to achieve a full understanding of itself and the nature of the world it inhabits. Yet although it may not be sufficient, it is certainly necessary: unless free play forms some part of the preschool child's day there is little chance of its acquiring the kind of knowledge about the world – both internal and external – from which real independence, or autonomy, develops. The child, in short, must be given the opportunity to develop for itself the desire to explore, invent, experiment; in fact to learn. Although skills can be taught, confidence, or motivation, or understanding can only be achieved.

From considering the varieties of relationship possible between the children and the adults in the nursery setting, it is perhaps natural to move on and ask more about the adults themselves. Who are they and where do they come from? What kind of job is it for them; what are its drawbacks or its rewards? How do they see their customers, the parents?

6

The job of caring

Who works in nurseries?

Of those who choose to work with children in day care by far the largest number are young girls in their late teens or early twenties who have started on the NNEB nursery nurse training as soon as they are old enough to do so, after leaving school. This category accounted for nearly 40 per cent of the staff at the nine nurseries we visited. A further 30 per cent approximately were people who had qualified in other related professions (such as education, nursing, residential child care) but had chosen to work in day nurseries. The remainder were either people with no qualifications or women who had done one or more of the courses run by the Preschool Playgroups Association.

The variety of routes into the profession was also reflected in the age structure. There were several older women who had either never married or had come back to work after their own children had grown up; there were very few younger married women with children of their own (except in the all-day playgroup); and there was a large number of much younger girls who had only recently left school. Two of the nurseries (Runnymede and Church Road) had made special arrangements to enable members of their staff who were married with children of their own to meet their family commitments, but this was not a regular feature in the nurseries we visited.

Looking at individual nurseries in more detail we found that the staffing ratios in the State nurseries tended to be more generous than those in the private nurseries. Whereas the average ratio of full-time staff to children at the State day nurseries was 1:4, in the private nurseries it ranged from 1:5 to 1:12 with an average of 1:7. (These figures relate to staff actually in employment when we visited the nurseries – some nurseries did have unfilled staff vacancies but they had not reduced the number of children catered for while waiting to fill a post.) The work-based nurseries tended to be less generously staffed than any of the others.

The differences between the staffing ratios at State and private nurseries are even more apparent when one looks at the importance of the training role in the State day nurseries. In addition to their very favourable ratio of *full-time staff* to children, two of the State nurseries also had a substantial quota of part-timers, in the form of NNEB students on day release (four girls at Paul Street and six at Church Road). More than 40 per cent of the adults present in the State day nurseries at any time were engaged in some sort of in-service training scheme – NNEB, PPA, child nursing or childcare. Only one of the private nurseries, Runnymede, had any staff who were attending training courses – two of their part-time staff were on a PPA training course. This nursery was almost entirely staffed by part-time helpers (there were five part-timers and one full-time organizer), but elsewhere part-time employment was not common. Excluding students, there were only five part-timers in the other private nurseries and three in the State day nurseries.

In the small sample we looked at not only did the State nurseries employ more staff they also employed more *qualified* staff. If those staff who were currently on day release were regarded as having already had some training, it was true to say that the State day nurseries employed no totally untrained staff. Only one of the private nurseries (Birkett) could match this record, and over all a third of the staff employed in private nurseries were unqualified. Whereas most of the nurseries employed people from a variety of backgrounds, at four of the nine nurseries we visited all the trained staff shared the same type of qualification. At Runnymede all the staff were playgroup trained; at Nightingale House it was nursery nurse training; at Marshall both the professional members of staff had been on residential child care courses; and at Wilberforce all the trained members of staff were teachers.

The quality of the staff being employed was not something that always came up as an issue of concern in the nurseries we visited. There is some evidence to suggest that the position that the nurseries find themselves in may be changing. Whereas before their low wages put them at a disadvantage, now there are many more people (particularly teachers) who are looking for jobs. The two nurseries (Vienna Close and Wilberforce) with the most coherent philosophies of how the children should be cared for were also most particular about the kind of staff they would employ. As the Organizer at Wilberforce said: 'We work very closely, it has to be someone we could all get on with.' She currently had one unqualified person on her staff and obviously found it not entirely satisfactory. 'She is good with the children but she lacks ideas; she is a bit stilted but she is willing to learn.'

Only one nursery was seriously concerned about the quality of their staff. Marshall Day Nursery employed three community service volunteers and the matron here expressed anxiety about leaving the children alone in the room with a community service volunteer who was not supervised. Other places also complained about the youth and inexperience of some of the nursery nurses they received. The size of a nursery is quite important in determining the *minimum* quality of staff which can be accepted without anxiety. In smaller institutions it is often necessary for every member of staff at some point to be left alone in charge of a group of children but in the larger day nurseries this can be avoided.

Various nurseries had had periods of crisis when many of their members of staff had left, but we did not get the impression that this was a general characteristic of the profession as a whole. Both Wilberforce and Church Road had had a big change when new organizers took over; Vienna Close was just about to have one because many of their trainees had come to the end of their course; and Marshall Day Nursery had regular changes of staff because the community service volunteers they employed were only on a three-month contract. Standards of what constituted stable employment varied from one institution to another. The Matron of Nightingale House felt that her nursery nurses tended to 'come and go' when two had stayed for eighteen months and one for three years. The supervisor of the factory nursery, on the other hand, considered that her staff had been there 'a long time' though only one out of five had been there for more than eighteen months. She did acknowledge that they had had some difficulty in staffing the nursery because their wage rates were low and there was plenty of alternative employment in the area. Whereas the State day nurseries tended to reduce the number of children on their books when they were understaffed, private nurseries did not appear to do so. Both Birkett and Nightingale House were looking for another member of staff when we visited them, but the 'temporary' situation at Birkett had persisted for two months and there were only two members of staff for 25 children.

The use of volunteers

The nursery staff tended to feel that volunteers were ill-prepared for the job they were going to do, they chopped and changed too often, and school children were often only there because it was a soft option for someone who could not think of anything 'better' to do. No nursery seemed to have been able to set up a system which involved adult volunteers coming in on a regular basis, except Vienna Close who had an Italian working there as part of her training course in child psychotherapy. Several places had had male students who had come for short periods, and had always been very welcome; but the majority of volunteers were schoolgirls. Understandably, the nurseries often tended to feel that they were being used as a resource, and got very little in return. We were told at Runnymede:

> 'One school sends three girls at a time and they only come for an hour which is not long enough to settle in. The other school sends groups of girls on Wednesday morning and Thursday afternoon. These girls who have been coming to the playgroup for some time are a great help, and will sit down at a table and talk to the children.'

The more effort the nursery is prepared to put into the task of creating a meaningful job for the volunteers the more likely it seems to be that both they and the children will benefit from it. Wilberforce had taken over the responsibility for preparing their volunteers. They always saw the girls before they came and they also insisted on talking to the teachers too to find out how the girls had been prepared before they started work with the children. They were told to watch the staff first and then they were given a particular activity to do with the children. Under these circumstances they were felt to be quite helpful.

It is interesting that although several of the nurseries we visited were run on a very tight budget, volunteers were not used to extend the service that these nurseries provided (except at Marshall where they used low-paid community service volunteers as part of the staff). There may be two reasons for this: firstly it is difficult to accommodate volunteers in a setting where even the professionals' training is considered by outsiders to be of a relatively low status; and secondly, the supervision of volunteers is itself a time-consuming activity which an overstretched organization can ill afford.

What kind of job is it?

We were frequently struck by how isolated the day nurseries were. Just as mothers caring for their children at home can find the demands of day-to-day care time-consuming and physically constraining, so can the staff of the day nurseries. The clearest case of this was at the university nursery where the staff found themselves isolated high up in a 'tower block' in a neighbourhood about which they knew very little and where they had no links with schools or local people. When there was a crisis, as when one of the members of staff went into hospital, it was to their own relatives that they turned for help in running the nursery. Small wonder that the girl who set this place up felt compelled after a couple of years to take a broader training which would give her more opportunities for a varied career.

The degree of contact which a nursery in the private sector has with the outside world seems to be a very personal matter, dependent to a large extent on the characteristics and interests of the person in charge. The Matron at Marshall Day Nursery, for example, knew very little about the area in which the nursery was situated and her only 'professional' link was with the funding charity which had no particular experience of caring for young children. The hospital crèche was equally isolated, but before taking over there, the Matron had had a much more varied career, and she had retained contact with people in related professions, such as teaching and day care, who provided a professional reference group for her. Of all the private nurseries we visited, Runnymede all-day playgroup seemed to be the least isolated and least like an institution. This was the only nursery which really arose out of local need (see Chapter 3) and the community, in the shape of the parents, still retained control over how the nursery was run. The Organizer was a very committed member of the playgroup movement and her staff were young mothers with children of their own either at the playgroup or attending local primary schools. We felt that the staff here were very much in tune with the parents whose children they were caring for, and through the playgroup courses and meetings (which three of them attended) they were also meeting other people in the same profession.

Of the three State day nurseries, Church Road probably had the most claim to being community-based. This was not because the community influenced how the nursery was run, but because the nursery endeavoured to be part of the community and not just an isolated institution. This meant encouraging visitors like the local policemen to come in and talk to the children; keeping in touch with parents who had left the nursery but still wanted to know what was going on; running a full programme of social activities for both parents and staff; and providing opportunities for both professional and ordinary people in the community to see what was going on in the nursery.

Job satisfaction is at least in part dependent upon having some idea about how your own task fits in with the whole, and some way of assessing whether or not you are doing it satisfactorily. In general the nurseries we saw tended not only to have few links with the local community but also to have poor links with other institutions concerned with the care of children.

This is a problem of which the Government is well aware. The DHSS and DES circular of January 1978 recommended the integration of the various different services for the under-fives (Paras. 15 & 16).

15 ... the Departments therefore hope that all authorities will examine the possibilities of improving the educational content of day care available in their areas. This could include the development of links between the education service and day centres and nurseries and playgroups as well as the special arrangements suggested for children in the care of childminders in para. 13 above. The best way forward may be to take education to the children by seeking to arrange for the nursery teachers to work directly with the children and those caring for them.

16 It is equally important that the desirability of linking the care, educational and health services for the three and four year

olds in areas of educational and social disadvantage should be recognized by authorities planning an expansion of nursery education so that these services are available for those children who need them most.

The lack of links with the educational system meant that the staff in most of the nurseries we visited had very little idea of what happened to their children after they left the nursery. They didn't know enough about how their part of the task fitted in with the whole to be able to assess whether or not they were producing 'competent and confident' children who were adapting well to the demands of primary school. (This was how a headmaster described the children who came on to him from Runnymede playgroup.) Some boroughs (and some charities) provide a supportive network for the organizers of their nurseries, and opportunities for them to meet people in the same or related professions, but many do not. They don't know how other people have tackled similar problems; they don't know how their standards of care and pattern of organization compare with those in similar institutions.

Out of the nine nurseries we visited, only four had managed to forge any kind of link with the local primary schools. Admittedly, this kind of arrangement is more difficult for some of the private nurseries, such as the university nursery which drew its children from a very wide catchment area, but it is possible, nevertheless. For example, one private nursery (Wilberforce) was prepared to spare a member of staff to go with parents when they went to register their children at whichever primary school they hoped to attend. One of the State day nurseries had a successful arrangement whereby fourteen of their children attended two classes at a local nursery school every afternoon; and they had also arranged exchanges of staff between the school and the day nursery. Those nurseries which had made contact with primary schools were also more likely to have good arrangements for the medical care of their children. Only four of the nurseries had regular medical checkups for their children and three of these were nurseries who also had links with the educational system. We felt that regular developmental health checks were an important service which nurseries ought to provide. Working parents have less time to take their children to a clinic and they may also have less idea of how their child is progressing compared with his contemporaries. Only one of the private nurseries had a proper health care programme with regular developmental checks, visits to the speech therapist and other specialist clinics at the hospital. The two standard State day nurseries had both got similar arrangements, and the third had previously had regular health checks for their children, though at the time of our visit the system had broken down because their doctor had left. Those nurseries which did offer a proper health care programme found that the staff as well as the parents could benefit tremendously from it: for the staff it was a valuable opportunity to see how other professionals coped with their children and to discuss any medical or psychological problems they had encountered, thereby gaining a broader perspective on the children in their care.

There was also considerable variation between nurseries in the extent to which they were aware of the home circumstances of their children. Wilberforce was the only private nursery which had arrangements for home visiting. Not surprisingly, the State day nurseries did better in this field, but even they were often hurt and bewildered by the casual way in which they were treated by the parents. Church Road, in particular, were distressed by the way in which some children who had spent several months in the nursery 'disappeared' without any leave-taking or discussion with the nursery staff.

The organizer's job

The degree to which the organizer's job differed from that of a nursery nurse or assistant depended to a large extent upon the size of the nursery. The management structure in the State day nurseries tended to be more elaborate than in the private nurseries. Most of the private nurseries were smaller with fewer members of staff and therefore could not support someone whose role was purely administrative. In the State day nurseries there was in every case an organizer and a deputy organizer. Of these two, one tended to be primarily responsible for relationships inside the nursery and its day-to-day running, while the other was primarily responsible for the external relationships of the nursery. These included liaison with the Social Services; finance and the purchasing of supplies; relationships with parents; liaising with social workers, medical authorities and schools. The organizers were responsible for all aspects of the nurseries' functioning and they had a high degree of autonomy within the financial constraints laid down by the Local Authority. Their financial position was of course a great deal more secure than that of most of the private nurseries.

The position of organizers in the private nurseries was somewhat different. Organizers in the smaller nurseries tended to have the widest range of responsibilities. Most of them spent the major part of their day working with the children but they were also responsible for the finance and administration of the nurseries. In both the larger private nurseries we saw – Nightingale House and Osborne Place – the organisers' responsibilities had been curtailed; finance and administration were handled by the employing institution. None of the private nurseries took upon themselves as much responsibility for the parents as the State day nurseries did (and dealing with parents can be a very time-consuming occupation!).

In three of the private nurseries we visited (Runnymede, Marshall and Birkett) it was clear that anxieties about the financial position of the nursery were a constant preoccupation for all the adults working there, though naturally the prime responsibility fell upon the organiser. People working in the State day nurseries or the work-based nurseries were luckier in this respect. Wilberforce too was currently well financed, but it would face a crisis when its grant came up for renewal.

The job of a nursery nurse or assistant

Though the nursery nurses, especially in smaller institutions, might share some of the worries and preoccupations of their senior staff, their job was primarily to look after the children. The way in which 'looking after the children' was interpreted varied considerably as Chapter 4 has shown. For some nursery nurses it involved never leaving the four walls of the day nursery for five days a week (Nightingale House and Osborne Place). For others where the staff shared a common outlook (and often a common training) the task might be rather different. At Wilberforce, for example, where most of the staff were teachers the day was organized very like a school day and in each activity the staff were expected to concentrate on extending the children's language, physical skills and grasp of concepts. At Vienna Close, on the other hand, where many of the staff were interested in child psychology, the emphasis was on developing social relationships and recreating home conditions as nearly as possible. Children and staff worked together on the ordinary household tasks, as the following observation shows.

> Before going out shopping some tidying was necessary.
> 'Dan, empty the bucket please. No, Joe, Dan's going to empty the bucket. If you need to wash your hands go into the bathroom, there's plenty of soap and there's a great big towel hanging on your peg.'
> 'This bucket is too heavy,' said Dan, tugging at its edge.
> 'Well, I'll tell you a secret,' said the staff member. 'Hold it by the handle, that's what it's for. And walk slowly and take little rests on the way.'

The nursery staff in the two work-based nurseries had less autonomy than in any of the other nurseries we visited. Although there were six members of staff at Nightingale House and five at Osborne Place there were no arrangements for staff meetings at either of these nurseries. At Osborne Place and Wilberforce the staff also had less freedom of action than elsewhere by virtue of the fact that there was a very carefully devised programme of activity worked out for the nursery as a whole. The State day nurseries tended to be larger than the private nurseries and were subdivided into family groups. The staff in charge of these family groups were responsible for organizing how their day should be spent.

The opportunity for developing meaningful relationships between staff and children will be relatively higher in a setting where working groups are smaller and the composition of the group is stable. There is therefore a *prima facie* case for regarding family grouping as being more satisfactory than age/ability grouping, particularly where the latter requires the adults to rotate between different age groups in the interests of providing them with a wider range of experience. The only nursery to mention any scheme that allowed adults to develop a special, individual relationship with one or two children was Paul Street; and even here it was not a general feature of the nursery's arrangements, but had been used to aid the transfer of one particularly difficult little boy from one family group to another.

Nearly every nursery we visited had staff meetings of some kind, but several nurseries had gone much further in trying to plan for the needs of the adults at the nursery. At Wilberforce there were regular coffee breaks and lunch-time meetings and a programme of outside visits each week. At Vienna Close the staff were being given the opportunity to work for a qualification as well as looking after the children, and individual interests and hobbies were not just tolerated but actively fostered, as a way of providing a richer environment for the children. The Organizer at Church Road said that many of her young staff had no social life other than that provided by the nursery in the form of discos, firework parties, cosmetic demonstrations. This same nursery also made a great effort to send its staff out during the daytime on courses or expeditions that would be of professional interest.

Sharing responsibility with the parents

Although one thinks of parents as the customers of the day nursery there is very seldom a straightforward contractual relationship between the nursery organizer and the parents. Frequently there is another agency which has some share in the relationship by virtue of controlling access to the nursery places or by financing the child while he attends the nursery. Children at the State day nurseries, Wilberforce and some of the children at the Marshall Day Nursery, had to be recommended for a place by social workers or medical practitioners. At the work-based nurseries, parents had to apply to their employer's personnel department to be put on the waiting list, and some recognition was made of the employer's need for different types of labour in allocating these nursery places which were in fact heavily subsidized. The very fact that nursery places are in such short supply must have some influence over the relationship between staff and parents, because the latter are only rarely in a position to pick and choose.

At the State day nurseries the majority of parents were not working, and this immediately distinguished them from the other institutions we saw, where the majority of mothers did work. The proportion of single parents too was much higher in the State nurseries: two of the private nurseries (Runnymede and Nightingale House) had no single parents at all. All the nurseries we visited had children with language problems of some kind, but in two, Osborne Place and Wilberforce, more than two-thirds of the children were foreign and many of them only used English as a second language.

The extent to which a nursery allows the parents to visit children at any time during the day is one measure of its attitude towards the parents. As a general guide, the work-based nurseries were less likely to allow unrestricted visiting. Marshall, Osborne Place and Nightingale House did not allow parents to visit their children during the day and they felt that this was in the best interests of the children. The rationale at Osborne Place was that visiting was unnecessary because many of their children had been to childminders before coming to the nursery. The majority would not be unhappy at parting anyway, and for those who were, it was only 'delaying the shock' which had to come even- tually. For a while they tried allowing mothers to come over and see their children at lunch time, but it proved impractical. Only some of the mothers came and the matron felt that this made the other children upset and jealous; and finally, since the mothers only had a very brief lunch break she felt there was not really enough time for a meaningful contact. This attitude was echoed at Nightingale House.

> 'If they could come and stay for two hours it would be different, but it doesn't really help the situation if they just pop in for a few minutes.'

Willingness to accept unscheduled parental visits could perhaps be taken as a measure of a nursery's willingness to share the responsibility for the care of the child.

At the other end of the scale, the three State day nurseries were working with women who were frequently going through a period of domestic crisis, and in contrast they were actually trying to persuade these mothers to spend more time in the nursery, to share responsibili- ty for the child. At Paul Street mothers were free to come in and see the children whenever they liked.

> 'The mums like it because they can come in and see the child whenever they like. The place is open. There are a lot of staff around, trained staff.'

From what has been said above it is quite clear that there are great differences in the degree to which nurseries accept responsibility for the *parents* of their children, as well as for the children themselves. Osborne Place and Nightingale House both saw their jobs as being much simpler than that of a conventional day nursery because they had no responsibility for the parents whatsoever. Theirs was simply a contractual arrangement to care for the children. As soon as you accept some local authority priority cases the ground shifts a little. The nurseries with a high proportion of children from a disturbed background all felt strongly that you cannot care for a child without caring for his parents too. This was the basic philosophy behind the setting up of Vienna Close.

> 'Our work should be involving the parents rather than excluding them or removing the children from them, and our method of treatment should be via relationship.'

The Organizer at Wilberforce explained why they felt they had to take responsibility for maintaining and enhancing the parent-child relationship.

> 'It is an important part of the job to try and improve the mother–child relationship. So often the parent's contact with the child is purely mechanical – they get the child up, dress it, feed it and hurry to bring it to the nursery. These are the kind of situations in which the adult is under pressure and the child is most likely to show disobedience.'

Occasionally there may be a danger that this concern for the parents can slip over into a benevolent paternalism, and how far this should go is open to conjecture. In some cases, it was clear that nurseries could be quite dictatorial about the advice they gave parents on how to handle their children, as this quotation from Nightingale House indicates.

> 'Sometimes we have to put right the feeding side of it, because we have the child four or five days a week and know what is happening.'

Our general impression (based only on the testimony of the staff not the parents) was that the nursery staff were very tolerant towards the parents in terms of what they expected the parents to do for the nursery. For example, despite the difficult financial position of the Birkett Nursery the parents had done no fund-raising, offered no help with mending the toys or doing the washing and quite often let the nursery staff down by failing to turn up for the parents' lunch-time rota. And yet the Organizer said: 'We don't expect them to do any more because they are working.' There was the same kind of tolerance at Runnymede.

> 'We have to give an awful lot to those mums – they've got a lot on their plate, and I know what it is like because I am working too.'

The use of 'tough' techniques to get the parents to cooperate was very rare – Wilberforce admitted to having sent out what the Organizer described as a 'nasty letter' telling parents that they were obliged to attend the four Open Evenings that are held each year, but that was the only instance of coercion we encountered.

Where parents did come into the nursery on a regular basis it was often because they needed help themselves. The organizer at one of the State day nurseries (Paul Street) described how they had a child in the babies' room whose mother was severely depressed. The mother came in twice a week with the child and stayed with him all day. At first she was unable to leave her child, but gradually she felt able to go off for an hour and do her shopping. The staff worked with the mother and tried to support her in the care of her child but they expected that eventually the baby would attend the nursery full-time. The organizer at another State day nursery talked about how helpful it was when they found they had got one or two coping parents amongst those they were catering for, whom they could actually involve in activities with the children, such as taking them to the library.

The question of what to do with parents who do offer to help is something which requires a certain amount of tact and organization. At Wilberforce the staff found that parents often seemed to find it easier to relate to other people's children in the nursery setting rather than their own. They would try to involve them in activities with another group of children, and to show them how to play with the children and enjoy them. Runnymede appeared to have more practical help from their parents than the other nurseries. They were the only nursery where the parents took a significant part in the management of the nursery and parents here also did some basic chores for the staff.

'We do insist that they help with the washing and ironing rota, though we understand they cannot come into the playgroup because they are working.'

Parental expectations of the nurseries seemed to fall into three categories, which sometimes overlapped. Three places – Birkett, Wilberforce and Nightingale House – mentioned that at least some of their parents saw the nursery as a preparation for school and hoped that their children would learn some of the basic preschool skills there. Other nurseries implied that many of their parents were so thankful to have their children off their hands and to know that they were properly cared for that they thought no further than that. We were told at Osborne Place:

'All they want to know is that we are here, that the nursery is professionally run, the staff are qualified, we supervise the children and we provide a safe and happy environment.

Finally, three of the nurseries felt that their parents were hoping for some kind of improvement in the relationships between themselves, their children and other adults. The Organizer of Paul Street said: 'They want to feel that people like their child; seeing his work on the wall shows that a child has been noticed and appreciated.' Other nurseries too mentioned how useful children's art work could be as a means of opening up a dialogue between the parents and the staff, or indeed between the parents and their own children.

The major way in which nurseries feel they are not fulfilling parents' requirements at present seems to be in their very limited capacity to cater for the under-twos.

Career prospects

It was not part of our brief to analyse the nursery nursing profession, and yet it was impossible to ignore the impact of defects in the professional structure upon the smooth-running of the nurseries.

Caring for the nation's under-fives is a critically important job which does not receive adequate recognition, whether it is done at home by a parent or childminder, or in an institution such as a school or a day nursery. Although most adults will have the experience of caring for one or more children at some stage in their lives this does not mean that such a relationship is so 'natural' that no training or preparation for it is required. Some recognition of the *breadth* of skills required from people employed in day care, particularly in State day nurseries, is contained in the DHSS/DES Circular of January 1978, paragraph 19:

> The priorities observed in allocating day nursery places have led to special problems in looking after the children, and also to much work having to be centred on the parents whose difficulties with child rearing may be compounded by low income, inadequate housing and lack of community support. The NNEB certificate, while giving trainees an excellent basic knowledge of normal child development does not fully prepare them for work with parents and with children who have multiple problems.

To what extent it is realistic to expect young girls in their late teens to be sufficiently mature to cope with these kinds of situations is open to question. What is clear is that the profession of day care lacks a proper career structure. The equivalence of different forms of training has not been worked out and there is a shortage of senior posts or opportunities to transfer sideways into related professions. The recent recommendation that senior staff appointed to day nurseries should hold social work qualifications will further reduce the opportunities for those with Nursery Nurse training, unless steps are taken to encourage them to obtain a further qualification by in-service training or secondment, such as a Certificate in Social Service or a Certificate of Qualification in Social Work.

Three of the most prevalent staffing problems mentioned by the organizers we spoke to were the problems of maintaining a balanced age structure in an individual nursery; the difficulty of persuading men to apply for posts in day care; and the problem of achieving any career progression for senior staff. The first two problems appear to be closely related to the latter. Teenage girls may look upon nursery nursing as a suitable short-term career because they expect to get married and give up work at least for a time, but boys have a different perspective. Vienna Close was the only place we visited which had male staff, and they were only there to gain practical experience before embarking upon a further qualification in child psychotherapy. Our interviews were full of stories of people who had either left the profession or were experiencing difficulties. The founder of Birkett Nursery left after two years to qualify as a social worker; the recently qualified teachers at Wilberforce were unable to count their experience at the nursery as a probationary year; the trainee mothers at Vienna Close had only managed to get a qualification which would be recognized in their own borough but not in any other borough.

Not many of the nurseries had a positive policy for staff development. This need not necessarily involve sending them on courses; a lot can be done within the normal running of the nursery to ensure that younger staff are exposed to new experiences. They can, for example, be given the opportunity to go with a child who needs to go to hospital or to the speech therapy clinic. Church Road kept a record for each member of staff of the visits they had made and courses they had attended. Wilberforce invited guest speakers to come and talk to all the staff during the lunch time break and, like Vienna Close, they had regular group sessions for members of staff to discuss problems with a child psychologist. At the simplest level, we felt that if staff were to keep a lively and active approach towards their job there needed to be some variety in the day-to-day programme of the nursery and in the physical setting of care. Outings, however brief, are important, as are visitors. They help to counteract some of the isolation of working in an institution with young children. Adults as well as children should find the nursery an interesting and stimulating place to be in.

7

The caretaking contract

We have been looking so far at what day nurseries, their children and their staff, are actually like: how they were started, how they are run, who attends them, what their inhabitants do all day, and the kinds of relationships they have with each other. Underlying our descriptions has been the fundamental issue of how it is that each nursery became the way it is; how it evolved its distinctive house style. What are the factors that are responsible, for instance, for one nursery's insistence upon formal instruction in numbers and colours and another's upon 'doing your own thing'? Why is it that some approach the day with the positive expectation of aims and intentions shared with the children and, at the very least, the possibility of a fruitful encounter with each other; and why on the other hand do others appear to brace themselves for an inevitable conflict of interests between adult and child and the constant vigilance necessary to stem the rising ride of chaos? No nursery at the outset, we assume, intends its day to be exhausting and unrewarding for staff or child. Yet in several of those we saw it appeared to happen. Of course, any nursery can have an off-day, produced by a number of uncontrollable factors: a member of staff away, for instance; even the weather can play its part. It is when the kind of day that is an exception for one nursery appears to be the rule for another that one needs to know more about the differences in their underlying structures and assumptions.

As we pointed out in Chapter 2, any organization concerned with the all-day care of young children must perform certain invarying functions if it is to operate with even minimal effectiveness. These include not only the provision of shelter, food, warmth, toilets, somewhere to run around, somewhere to rest, toys and other equipment, but also certain less tangible functions that may be just as significant for the child's, and hence the nursery's survival. These have to do with the establishment of a community in which both child and adult can feel themselves to play a part; with the acquisition of competences that are relevant not only to the child's life both in and out of the nursery, but also to the next stage in his life cycle; with the provision of a basis for some sort of a relationship between each child and the adults who care for him.

In this final chapter we speculate upon the factors that can lead different nurseries to manifest these functions – perhaps in particular the less tangible ones – so very differently; for Wilberforce Nursery to place the emphasis upon 'teaching' those skills they felt to be significant and for Vienna Close merely, as it were, to provide the opportunity for learning.

In fact as we look back at our nurseries, we see a major division between those whose daily programme gave weight to cognitive skills and those which felt that social and emotional development was of prime importance. We do not suppose that those nurseries where the emphasis was upon cognitive development would for an instant deny the significance of social and emotional factors; we are commenting only upon the relative prominence given to each objective within their daily routine. Those nurseries where there was an emphasis upon the formal aspects of education, as revealed by the existence of 'lessons', or sessions in which the children had no choice in whether they attended and what they did during these periods, included Nightingale House, Osborne Place, Wilberforce and Marshall. Those nurseries that had no formal lesson sessions and expressed a primary concern with the children's abilities to form satisfactory social relationships were the three State nurseries plus Runnymede and Birkett.

We suggest that the choice of primary goal is a decision that has far-reaching consequences for the pattern of the nursery day. Even if it is never explicitly formulated, once the decision has been made in favour of cognitive, rather than social or emotional goals, certain things will follow automatically.

In order for the staff to feel that they are fulfilling their role as educators there must be formalized opportunities for them to 'teach'. Material must be taught that is easily testable, perhaps accounting for the popularity of numbers and colours; sessions of this kind will require silence, or at any rate a low noise level; the language sanctioned within such a session will be related to the task in hand (the child's explanation of who it is who will be taking him to school in place of his dead father is ignored in favour of further repetition of the date and weather); behaviour from the adults will be 'restricting', since it is geared to getting the children to accomplish the task in hand and cannot allow for deviations (circles for balloons cannot become an owl); moreover the behaviour of a teacher is perceived as distinct from that of a mother, whose role is comforting, supporting and tolerant rather than stimulating, directional and restrictive.

Similarly, once the primary goal has been defined (again however implicitly) as social and emotional development, then certain things will follow. The bulk of the child's day will be spent in groups whose composition and size will be of his own choosing. Sometimes these will accumulate around a specific activity provided by the adult (for example, the tissue paper collage described on pages 44 and 45) and sometimes they will form spontaneously outside the confines of a planned activity, in the Wendy House or out-of-doors. A certain level of noise will have to be tolerated, since relationships are rarely conducted in silence; language about the self and inner states, the subjective reality of an experience is permitted, even encouraged – the sandcastle can become a delicious apple pudding. Behaviour from the adults can be permitting, and cooperative towards ends selected by the child. Mothering, rather than teaching, is the model for staff behaviour: the kind and degree of tolerance, contact and support offered is related to the needs of that child at that moment.

Why, one might ask, is it not possible for these goals to be achieved simultaneously? Why should not the development of the ability to form satisfying social relationships proceed within the framework of a fairly formal structure to a day in which specific skills are imparted? Similarly, why should not the conventional skills be picked up more or less along the way during the rough and tumble of a less structured nursery day? In both cases, the answer is that to some extent both are possible. In the average family that is precisely what happens. But nursery life is not like family life: on the whole nurseries *do* behave as though they had some end in view, as though a definable goal were expected of them. We do not ask mothers what their aims and objectives are as they sit in the park with their offspring, perhaps because (having no choice in the matter) we trust them to be sufficiently well-disposed to their children and to know them sufficiently well to be the best judge of their needs at any one moment. But nurseries cannot deal with one child at a time. An individual's needs may be at odds with those of the majority (although he may be 'ready' to learn to sort out the block-posting box this afternoon, right now he needs a cuddle); it simply is not possible within large groups of children, where the adult/child ratio may on some days be as high as 1 : 12, to spend that amount of time with any one child. Consequently the nursery has to make some decisions about priorities, and hence programmes.

Thus the decision for a nursery to concentrate primarily upon either social or cognitive goals is a very major determinant of the 'house style': the way the day will be spent and hence experienced by the child and adult. Are there other equally important decisions to be made (and again we are not assuming that all decisions have to be either conscious or overt) which will have equally far-reaching consequences for the style and content of day nursery life?

We feel that there is a second such decision which has far-reaching implications for nursery life, although it is formulated as less of a goal than an underlying assumption. We are referring to the differing views that nurseries hold about the nature of the child as a species; not necessarily explicitly again, but as revealed (see Chapters 3 and 5) in what each nursery sees as its role, or its aims and objectives. Here the distinction is between whether it is to be the *child* or the *adult* who decides what in a given setting the child should be doing. We do not say that any nursery we visited acted either as though 'the child knows best' or 'the adult knows best' was an unbreakable rule; again, it was a question of emphasis as revealed in staff attitudes to the children in their care. If we look back at our nine nurseries and their expressed opinions as to their aims and objectives we can see a possible classification into, broadly speaking, 'child-centred' establishments and 'adult-centred' establishments.

Child-centred	*Adult-centred*
Paul Street	Nightingale House
Church Road	Osborne Place
Vienna Close	Marshall Day Nursery
Birkett Nursery	Wilberforce Nursery
Runnymede	

Again, the underlying assumption was associated with other features within the running of the nursery day. If the child is to be considered a thinking, feeling individual with needs and attitudes of its own, it follows that one cannot think of the adults as being any less autonomous than the children in their charge. Consequently, child-centred establishments were associated with *democratic* styles of house management, in which adults were given considerable independence over how they organized their room or their group. Again, a child-centred approach to the nursery day virtually committed an organization to 'free play' in that the bulk of the day would be spent in activities of the child's choice. With a commitment to free play, goes, as we have already spelled out, rather more noise, 'permitting' rather than restricting adults, language other than that strictly relevant to the task in hand, and the chance for the child to resolve some of its own inevitable conflicts with its peers. The extent of the child's freedom is of course only relative, since the materials, toys and equipment present in any nursery are the result of adult decisions. Again, it is a question of emphasis.

In contrast, if the underlying assumption is that the adult is the only appropriate determiner of what is in the child's best interests, it follows that junior staff will be regarded as inevitably less competent than more senior staff; and the nursery will manifest a *hierarchic* system of management, with instructions as to the form and content of the children's day tending to come from above. The bulk of the child's day will be spent in adult-initiated and adult-directed behaviour, with, as we have already described, all that that implies in terms of restrictions upon the children's behaviour, language and freedom of choice.

What restrictions will a hierarchic management structure impose upon the staff themselves? Once the initiative in determining the course of the day is removed from a member of staff she becomes someone whose role is merely to perform tasks set for her by someone else; she belongs in effect to a special category of larger child. She becomes someone whose job it is to see that the smaller children in her charge conform to a schedule; and inevitably the children will be responded to in terms of how well or poorly they conform to that schedule. Thus not only will the children be assessed by how receptive they are to doing what they are told, but it may be hard for the staff-member engaged in doing what *she* has been told to feel any real responsibility for the consequences of what she does. A hierarchic management structure has far-reaching significance for child and adult alike.

If we now attempt to classify our nurseries in terms of firstly their *underlying assumptions* and secondly their *goals*, we can perceive groupings emerging.

Table 1

Predominant goals	Underlying assumptions	
	Child as major determiner of what will satisfy its needs	*Adult as major determiner of what will satisfy child's needs*
Social and emotional development	Paul Street Church Road Vienna Close Birkett Nursery Runnymede Play Group	
Cognitive growth and acquisition of skills		Nightingale House Osborne Place Wilberforce Nursery Marshall Day Nursery

Is it impossible to have as one's primary goal the development of social and emotional behaviour if one also happens to believe that the adult knows best what is good for the child? Not at any rate in theory; but in practice, particularly with very young children, the means will be antithetical to the ends, as any two mothers who have tried to get their respective offspring to become friends know very well. Why, in the same way, is the assumption that the child is the most appropriate determiner of its own needs apparently incompatible with a predominating goal of the development of cognitive skills? The answer here lies, we think, in the word predominant: those nurseries who place social and emotional goals first do so because they feel that in terms of the child's long-term success as a cognitive being, a sound emotional basis is essential.

Where do these underlying assumptions and these primary goals come from? Are they articulated at any point in the origins and development of each nursery? At what point is the step taken that commits a nursery to one path or to the other?

As to their origins, as we indicated in Chapter 3, historically there have been two traditions from within which pre-school care has developed. On the one hand were those establishments concerned with the care of children of the poor and of working women. The early dame schools were primarily concerned with keeping children off the streets, and weaning them away from, or preventing them from developing, bad habits. The theme of rehabilitation was predominant, and perhaps reflected in an attitude still to be heard expressed, most succinctly in Nancy Astor's comment that it is cheaper to have nursery schools than prisons; and more traditionally by the proverb 'prevention is better than cure'.

The second route stems from the development of the recognition of the importance *for the child* of the early years of life, and has its expression in the development of progressive nursery education; of the recognition of the child as an individual with potential for autonomously motivated and constructive behaviour. Here the emphasis was upon providing an environment in which this potential might develop fully. The adult's role here is seen in terms of cooperating with the child's needs and assisting with his ambitions, rather of controlling, usually by frustrating, those same needs and ambitions. In many respects the division between these two approaches to child care is perpetuated by the division of responsibility between the DHSS, under whose aegis comes day care, and the DES, which is responsible for nursery education. More recently, an attempt to coordinate services provided by the DHSS and DES has resulted in the establishment of 'combined centres' which formally combine the functions of care and education. However, looking back at some of the day nurseries we visited, it is hard not to feel that there existed a continuity of tradition between the dame schools, in which the emphasis was upon keeping children out of mischief, and those we saw in which, as we have described, the children were felt to be primitive and irrational creatures to be kept carefully and constantly controlled by the adult world.

We can perceive a similar continuity of tradition between early nursery education, in which the importance of the child itself was the rationale for the nursery's activities, and those establishments in which the development of the child's own interests is encouraged and valued: the child-centred establishment.

Related to these historical attitudes, and exhibiting a similar polarity of approaches, are the rationales behind the setting up of the nurseries we visited, described in detail in Chapter 3. On one side are those nurseries which are available only to a distressed sector of society, where the provision of care is free once the applicant has demonstrated she is sufficiently needy to warrant it. Contrasted with this as a reason for existence is the more recent feeling that nursery care for the under-fives should be available to all as of right, for parents to take advantage of as and when they choose. A few experimental nursery centres currently exist in London (Thomas Coram, Maxilla, Dorothy Gardiner) for anyone within a certain catchment area to use on demand; but of the nurseries we visited only Birkett and Runnymede had their origins in the belief that any woman who so chooses has a right to a life outside the home.

The third group of nurseries, that which included Nightingale House and Osborne Place, had a straightforwardly commercial rationale in that they existed to make it possible for women to work full-time in the establishments to which they were attached; they were thus providing a service that in some respects linked the two rationales for existence just described: they were provided for the children of working women, although there was some evidence that not all the women using these two nurseries worked for financial reasons alone.

We will leave for the moment the question of the point at which, during the setting up of the nursery, the decision is made as to the predominant goal. Instead we turn back to the issue raised in Chapter 5: what is life in the day nursery like for the child? In particular, what is it like in a nursery operating under the conditions produced by the two underlying assumptions we have outlined? In which nurseries did we find positive alliances between adult and child and in which nurseries did negative alliances occur most frequently? The list merely repeats the basic division we have already drawn up in the Table on page 111: nurseries with a child-centred approach, and with social and emotional goals predominating, are those whose practices result in a positive alliance with the children in their charge. Nurseries with an adult-dominated approach, and cognitive goals as their predominating aim, are those in which negative alliances tend to occur.

We can now summarize the clustering of features in the nurseries visited in the following way. When the *underlying assumption* is that the child is a thinking, feeling individual with needs, attitudes and opinions of its own, the nursery's *predominant goal* is likely to be enabling the development of satisfying social and emotional relationships. In *practice*, this will be manifested in a number of ways, of which the most obvious are a democratic system of management for the staff, and a day in which the larger part will be spent in 'free play': that is, in an activity and with the companions of the child's choice. The predominant style of control will be *cooperative* and the 'permitting' rather than the 'restricting' style of adult will be apparent. There will be plenty of children's work on the walls (not necessarily very elegantly displayed) in keeping with the nursery's appreciation of the child's productions as expressions of its self. The day may be a fairly noisy one, but within the bustle will be heard language about things other than the task in hand; about the self, about feelings and inner preoccupations as well as language designed to get things done. Some of the noise may include the overt expression of conflicts between the children (although they will be separated if they come to blows). There will be no specific periods of the day called 'lessons' and much of the equipment and the uses to which it is put will be improvised. There will be physical contact between the adults and children for other than merely caretaking purposes: gestures of comfort, or affection. In summary, these features are both cause and effect of what we have called *a positive alliance*.

In contrast is the kind of nursery that maintains a *negative alliance*. Here the *underlying assumption* that the child is a primitive chaotic creature until controlled and shaped by the adults' superior strength and wisdom is associated with a *predominant goal* of promoting cognitive growth and the acquisition of skills. This will be manifested *in practice* by a hierarchic staff management system, and a day in which the child spends most of its time in a group whose size, composition and goal are determined by the adults. A *confronting* style of control will predominate, and adults will tend to be restricting rather than permitting in function. Since the child's productions are valued only in so far as they approach adult standards, only 'good' work will appear on the walls; occasionally some of this will have been done by the adults themselves. There will be frequent attempts to reduce or eliminate noise altogether, with varying success. Language between adult and child will be restricted to the task in hand; if an argument develops between children it will be cut short by the nearest adult.

There will be parts of the day set aside for 'lessons' or the teaching of specific skills; the equipment in the nursery will be bought and used only for the purpose for which it was originally designed. It will be very rare to see physical contact between adults and children for anything other than caretaking purposes: feeding, washing and clothing.

It should not be, at least in theory, an impossible task to care lovingly and constructively for someone else's child, and one might imagine that the more regular the basis on which it occurred the easier it would be. Yet in practice it often turns out to be remarkably difficult. Why should this be so? Does it turn only upon the question of the goals a nursery is pursuing, or the assumption underlying its operation? It seems unlikely that this alone can be the answer. As we have already indicated, the critical feature of the child's day, determining more than any other the quality of its experience, is the nature of its relationships with the staff. These, as we have seen, ranged from the rigid, controlling and authoritarian to the flexible, empathic and tolerant. Yet can it be that only flexible and empathic staff are employed by fundamentally child-centred establishments and that adult-centred nurseries develop an unerring eye for the rigid and authoritarian personality? Is it, in fact, that certain kinds of staff are attracted to certain kinds of nurseries; or is it rather that the house style – once established – is so pervasive that staff find themselves conforming, whatever their individual inclinations? The younger and less experienced the staff, perhaps, the more likely it is that their individual styles or convictions will become adapted to the prevailing attitudes in the nursery, for good or ill. If true, this might make the placement of students a matter for the most careful consideration; no amount of theoretical advice on how to comfort a child distressed by separation could prevail against a superior who decided that a child who cried was hungry, tired or merely naughty, and who treated it accordingly.

Several nurseries (Vienna Close, Church Road, Wilberforce) made explicit efforts to find staff whose own convictions fitted in with the nursery's existing philosophy. Vienna Close was clearest about the importance for the nursery as a whole of doing this: they felt the rewards in terms of harmonious staff-staff and staff-child relationships justified the wait for the right person to come along, even if it meant limiting the number of children cared for until that happened. What Vienna Close was searching for, however, was a personality and a style of behaviour; Wilberforce, who were also clear about the type of staff it wanted, were in search of professional qualifications. These differences were reflected in the goals articulated by the two nurseries. In Vienna Close, the relationships were seen as the foundation stone for whatever else might be going to happen; in Wilberforce, cognitive growth and development came first.

One possibility to be considered is that whatever the qualifications they may have acquired, many people who enter the field of child care are in fact unsuited to it. It is an extremely demanding and arduous job, both physically and emotionally, and the rewards, whether financial, in terms of social status or career structure, are still, regrettably, absolutely minimal. Exactly the same might be said of motherhood itself, of course – but with motherhood there is the pleasure and satisfaction of knowing that you are caring for your own offspring in the way you believe it should be done. Yet, if the caretaker has entered the field for its emotional rewards, since there seem to be few others, will she not be in for something of a disappointment? For unlike motherhood, caring for someone else's toddler carries with it the permanent conviction that the caretaker can only ever, at best, be a substitute for 'the real thing'. Moreover, the sensitive and scrupulous caretaker may well feel obliged to remain second-best, tacitly recognizing that it could create an insoluble dilemma for the child should its attachment to the temporary caretaker become stronger than that to its permanent parent.

The long-term effects of such a conviction are perhaps incalculable. It is not hard to imagine its driving many young women prematurely into starting families of their own. It must surely take adults of the greatest maturity and integrity to enjoy children enough to want to do the job and yet to be able to meet the child's needs without being tempted to replace the parent. But the fact is that as a nation we rate the job of child care very poorly indeed – as an eminently suitable career for any adolescent girl with a minimal academic record and an expressed desire 'to work with children'. Sometimes it will be her own needs that are paramount in her choice of job, rather than the child's. We clearly cannot select for the job of motherhood itself, but we can and must select for the job of caring; if motherhood is seen as a demanding job, how much more so should we consider the care of other people's children, providing as it does quite as many of the burdens with rather fewer of the pleasures?

Yet it is too easy to blame the failures of so many staff members to achieve a positive alliance with the children in their charge upon the individual's training, or indeed her personality problems. It might conceivably be, to look at the problem from another point of view altogether, that under certain conditions, caring for other people's children all day long can produce tensions in the staff which rebound upon the children in their care.

We use the notion of a *caretaking contract* to describe the framework within which the daily relationship between the three parties – staff, parent and child – is operating. Such a contract exists from the moment the child enters the nursery's care, whether for good or bad. To understand the forms this contract can take, we must retrace our steps to the point at which we were discussing rationales for existence. Here we can see that the three State nurseries, operating as they do upon the premise that only the neediest and most distressed of parents qualify for their assistance, are in fact offering a style of contract that differs in some important respects from that offered by private nurseries. State nurseries exist to help mothers and children whose own relationships have broken down for either practical or emotional reasons. They therefore set out to provide an environment in which the mother is given both practical help, and emotional support, in the form of accepting and non-judgemental care for her child; and for her too, if she feels able and inclined to accept it. These nurseries' main goals are in some way related to the breakdown of the parent-child relationship, and their emphasis, if articulated at all, is connected with the repair and maintenance of these emotional ties. They place less value upon the more formal aspects of education since they feel it to be irrelevant at that point in the child's career.

In the State system therefore, parent, nursery and child all have roles that are equally crucial in the contract. The nursery regards the mother and the child as a unit. Although the bulk of the realization of the contract takes place between nursery and child, care and attention for the child is also seen as being care and attention for the mother.

Very important, perhaps critically important, in enabling the nursery to adopt such a caring role, is the tacit admission on the part of the parent from the moment he or she enters the nursery that she is in desperate need of help. The nursery is enabled by that admission to accept that need and pledge a supportive role. The nursery does not attempt to replace the mother, neither does it intend (although in extreme cases it may be necessary) to provide compensatory care. Its eventual aim is to enable the mother to do for her own child what the nursery does. Because it is not attempting to replace the mother, conflicts over goals for the child are less likely to occur.

In the independent nurseries, on the other hand, in the majority of cases the relation between parent and nursery is one of choice rather than need; and the contract is accordingly more complex. Independent nurseries existed for a variety of reasons, ranging from the self-interest of an employer to the benevolent preoccupation of a charitable institution. There may be parents with children in independent nurseries who are in as desperate straits as those with children in State nurseries, but the admission of such need does not generally form part of the caretaking contract in the independent nursery. The contract here is based upon *substitution for* the mother, rather than an *alliance with* her. The tacit admission upon entry to the nursery is not 'I cannot cope,' but something rather less submissive, more along the lines of 'For one reason or another I choose not to look after my child during the day. I will pay you to do it for me.' The contract here is not acted out through the medium of the child for the equal benefit of parent, child and nursery, but rather negotiated solely between parent and nursery for their own respective advantages; and the child becomes merely the passive recipient of the consequences of that contract.

In the contract with the State nursery, the assumption from the outset is that the child as well as the parent benefits from his being admitted to the nursery, but in the independent forms of day care no such satisfying conclusion can automatically be reached. Here, to put it bluntly, it may not be in the child's best interests to be in day care.

What effect does this lack of a clearly justifiable role have upon the staff in such nurseries? In place of the conviction that one is performing a necessary and valuable service is the feeling that one is doing someone else's job and being very poorly rewarded for it. Envy of the parent thus freed from the burdens of her role can produce resentment and hostility, and hence guilt – all of them likely to be expressed, however unintentionally, within the caretaker's relationship with the child. What, in brief, is being suggested, is that one of the critical factors in enabling an institution to adopt successfully the role of the parent (whether in addition to or as a substitute for that parent), both institution and parent must be separately and equally convinced that it is in the child's interests to be cared for in this way. Where there is ambiguity or ambivalence, the tensions these create can rebound upon the child in care. A liberated parent can be in danger of handing her child over to a caretaker considerably less far along the path to women's rights than she may be herself.

This lack of an explicit and sufficient (from the staff's point of view) reason for the child's being in independent day care is, we suggest, at the heart of the emphasis upon the formal aspects of education that was so marked in all but two of the independent nurseries we saw. Since a parent cannot always justify in terms of desperate need handing her child over to a substitute, there is some pressure for her to believe that the nursery is doing a better job with the child than she herself could possibly achieve; and in the same way, and for the same reasons, since the nursery may be unclear about the precise justification for mothering someone else's child, they too are relieved of the pressure of judging the parent by feeling they are giving the child something that the parent is unable to provide. (The potency of such 'judgements' in affecting behaviour is undiminished by the fact that they may be unconscious.) Education, universally recognized as desirable, highly prized by every sector of society, of undeniable value both personally and professionally, would seem to fit the bill admirably. Hence, we suggest, the organization of many independent nurseries upon lines more suited to the primary school.

With this hypothesis in mind, it is interesting to speculate upon the incident at Nightingale House, described on pages 66–7. The overfeeding of the infant could be seen in this instance to play the same role that we have suggested education plays in the care of the older child. The nursery is perceived by the uneasy parent to be giving the child something she herself is unable to bestow: 'How much better he's sleeping now he's on solids,' replaces 'He knows all his colours and he's only two.' Cereals are taking the place of facts, yet both are in fact premature. They are useful primarily as comforters·or pacifiers for both parent and staff, enabling them to regard the child as being in the care of 'experts' who do 'better' than the parent in one respect or another.

However, two of the independent nurseries we saw appeared to have negotiated a successful contract, in that the alliance between staff and children was positive, there was no insistence upon the formal aspects of education, nor was there any obvious feature of the nursery day that substituted for education as a hallmark of the 'expertness' of the care received.

In Birkett Nursery, to be sure, education played a part in that it was seen as sufficient justification for leaving the child in care; but it was the education of the *parents* rather than the children. Moreover it was sessional care (having a place did not oblige a child to attend full-time) and thus for many was part-time even during term. From the parents' point of view, the care provided by Birkett had more in common with that provided by a playgroup or a nursery school, rather than a day-nursery; and this view was supported by the absence in this nursery of certain traditional day-nursery features, such as the afternoon rest and the provision of the midday meal. (The parents themselves were responsible for lunch.)

The other independent nursery to have negotiated a successful contract had adopted a strategy that in some ways was similar to Birkett's, although it had gone even further. Runnymede Playgroup provided day-care, but it was an organization for which the parents themselves took the responsibility. No-one is better qualified to understand the endless demands made by small children on young parents than other young parents; no-one is less likely to feel ambivalent about a parent wanting to share the burdens of caring for a child than another parent with the same end in view. By retaining the responsibility for the organization that cared for their children, Runnymede's parents had succeeded in eliminating the ambiguities and tensions of the independent nurseries' caretaking contract. The nursery in fact belonged to the parents, and their commitment to it enabled both parties to feel that they were contributing towards a common goal; neither's role was undervalued by the other. We suggest that to share the responsibility for the maintenance of the caretaking contract is likely to be an effective way of ensuring that it operates in the child's interests. Such a principle is of course well known, and many nurseries expressed the desire for more parent involvement. However, involvement is not enough: it is the shared *responsibility*, with the mutual respect that this implies, that makes for a successful caretaking contract.

The interrelation between, on the one hand, the (often unspoken) philosophy and historical derivation of a nursery and, on the other, the manner in which it relates to the children in its charge, their parents, and its own staff, are summarized in Table 2.

What can we say, in summary, about the successes and failures in day care? We have not attempted to discuss the fundamental issue of whether or not the day nursery is the best place to care for the young child away from its mother. The practicalities of the situation are that there will always be women who, for whatever reason, do not stay at home with their young children, and there will always be people who respond to their need, whether for commercial gain, for reasons of altruism or as part of the philosophy of the Welfare State. Our interest has been in looking at the styles of response currently available from the point of view of the preschool child himself, the victim or the beneficiary of whatever treatment he receives. How can we increase the chances of establishing a successful working relationship between parent, caretaker and child?

Firstly, we feel, the success of the contract to care for some one else's child depends upon the adults on both sides having acknowledged to themselves and clarified between each other the nature of the job that is to be done, and its justification. In many situations this is done for them by a particular nursery's admissions policy: where, as we have said, a nursery will only accept the children of mothers in desperate need, the nature of the contract has already been spelled out. It is where substitute care is undertaken for other reasons that all parties need to be clear about the justification for their respective roles. Residual conflicts and uncertainties will only rebound upon the children themselves.

Secondly, and intimately connected with a clearsighted understanding of the adults' roles, it is important to understand the nature of the care appropriate for children of different ages and stages. Although it is recognized that the needs of infants differ from those of toddlers to the extent that it is impossible to meet these different needs in an institutional setting without a very high staff-child ratio, we would argue that the needs for a two-year-old differ by an equally great amount from those of a rising-five about to find himself in the reception class at primary school; the education appropriate for one group will differ enormously from that suitable for the other. That some form of educa-

Table 2

UNDERLYING ASSUMPTION A (Historical tradition: progressive nursery education)	UNDERLYING ASSUMPTION B (Historical tradition: dame schools and rehabilitation of poor)
Child is thinking, feeling individual with needs, attitudes, opinions of own. Is capable of *internal* controls in regulating own behaviour	Child is ignorant of what is best for it; own feelings and attitudes lead to chaos unless behaviour controlled *externally* by adult world
Hence adults viewed in same light, leading to DEMOCRATIC management structure	Hence junior staff less competent than senior leading to HIERARCHIC management structure
Parents seen as equal partners in caretaking enterprise; frequent contact	Parents play unequal role in caretaking enterprise

MANIFESTATION OF A

↓

House style

'Free play', i.e. child chooses what, when, how and with whom it plays for bulk of the day

Child's productions valued as expressions of self, hence much work on wall

'Permitting' adults and cooperative style of control

Noisy

Overt expression of conflict, hostility permitted

Expressive as well as transactional language

Improvization of equipment and uses to which it is put

Physical contact between adults and children for other than care-taking purposes

No explicitly educational sessions e.g. 'lessons'

TOTAL = POSITIVE ALLIANCE

MANIFESTATION OF B

↑

House style

Adult-determined activity for bulk of day: staff initiated and staff controlled

Child's productions valued in as much as they approach adult standards, hence only 'model' works on walls

'Restricting' adults and confronting style of control

Frequent attempts to lower noise level

Overt expression of hostility not permitted

Language mainly transactional

Equipment bought, and used only for purpose for which designed

Little physical contact between adults and children for other than caretaking purposes

'Lessons' or other activities for specifically educational purposes

TOTAL = NEGATIVE ALLIANCE

Parents use nursery because
either or

Needy/distressed

Role: show parents how to do it *or* do it for them if they are really incapable

Not needy; child in daycare from parents choice

Role: unclear

Needy/distressed

Role: caretaking staff know better than parents; paternalistic and moralistic attitudes

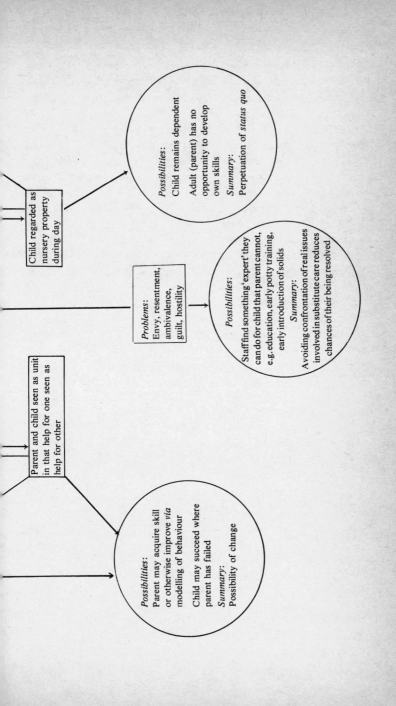

Child regarded as nursery property during day

Possibilities:
Child remains dependent

Adult (parent) has no opportunity to develop own skills

Summary:
Perpetuation of *status quo*

Parent and child seen as unit in that help for one seen as help for other

Problems:
Envy, resentment, ambivalence, guilt, hostility

Possibilities:
Staff find something 'expert' they can do for child that parent cannot, e.g. education, early potty training, early introduction of solids

Summary:
Avoiding confrontation of real issues involved in substitute care reduces chances of their being resolved

Possibilities:
Parent may acquire skill or otherwise improve *via* modelling of behaviour

Child may succeed where parent has failed

Summary:
Possibility of change

tion, in its very broadest sense, is desirable for both groups is undeniable. What is even more important is that education in the narrow sense – the naming of parts, or the rote learning of numbers and colours – is not merely a justification or a rationalization for taking over the daytime care of the child. Before the goals of cognitive growth and development can be pursued there must be a firm foundation of confidence and emotional stability, as any primary school teacher will confirm. Indeed so intimately connected are emotional security and cognitive growth in the earliest years that it is fair to regard them as one; to attempt to teach a child preoccupied with the instability of its home life to recite numbers up to twenty will be counterproductive. For these reasons, and bearing in mind the fact that existing day nursery populations are likely to be those most at risk in these areas, we feel it is not too broad a generalization to claim that the *primary* goal of the day nursery should be to establish a climate within which the 2, 3 or 4 year old child can achieve the satisfactions of his emotional and social requirements. It should not be forgotten that the average child within a day nursery spends a much longer time away from home than he will once he is at primary school; and even at primary school, the proportion of the day devoted to formal learning will be relatively small. How much more suitable, therefore, is 'home' as a model for the day nursery day rather than 'school'.

Intimately connected with the identification of the primary goal of emotional stability is the underlying assumption that allows the child to determine the pattern of its day, rather than the adult. Indeed, so closely connected are the two goals with the two basic assumptions that it is impossible, and perhaps even unnecessary, to say which comes first. However, a child-centred approach to the day virtually commits the organization to a democratic management style, with beneficial repercussions for staff as well as children, as we suggested earlier.

The third issue is that of the selection and training of staff, discussed in some detail in Chapter 6. Clearly it is important to improve the status of the profession, both for the sake of those who are currently working in day nurseries and to ensure that recruits of adequate calibre are attracted to them. The desire to 'work with children' is no longer, as it has tended to be, sufficient justification for training. We need to know more about the factors in an individual's background that have produced this desire, and we need an effective system for diverting misfits. Looking after other people's children is in many ways more taxing than looking after one's own; moreover the job of working in a nursery requires other important skills, including the willingness and the ability to understand parents' predicaments and to work with them in a spirit of cooperation rather than rivalry. The maturity of outlook which this necessarily involves leads one to suggest that the selection and training of nursery nurses should be carefully scrutinized, and the opportunities for older men and women to join the profession should be increased.

Fourthly, there is the question of the isolation of the day nursery from the outside world, a problem equally great for staff and children. Isolation is well documented as a cause of depression and deprivation for mothers with young children. Why should we assume that it will cause any less of a problem for adults with many young children in their care? A support system must be not only a means of getting help from the outside world in the form of visits from medical staff, speech therapists, psychologists and welfare officers, but also a source of stimulation, of ideas, of reactions to what the nursery has done that day; a means of meshing that nursery into the larger community in such a way that it feels itself to play a significant part in the formation of that same community.

There is every reason to suppose, following much observation and research, that young children need not be damaged, either emotionally or intellectually, by good substitute care. We also have at this point a growing knowledge of some of the factors that contribute to the success or failure of such care. We really no longer have any excuse for permitting less than the very best to continue in practice. Taking good care of our children is, quite apart from its intrinsic satisfactions, a very real investment in our own futures as well as theirs.

Short bibliography

BONE, M. (1976) Day care for preschool children. In *Low Cost Day Provision for Under Fives*. Papers from a conference held at the Civil Service College, Sunningdale. London: DHSS and DES.

BOWLBY, J. (1953) *Child Care and the Growth of Love*. Harmondsworth and New York: Penguin.

BROWN, G. W. and HARRIS, T. O. (1978) *Social Origins of Depression*. London: Tavistock; New York: Free Press.

CENTRAL POLICY REVIEW STAFF (1978) *Services for Young Children with Working Mothers*. London: HMSO.

DEPARTMENT OF EDUCATION AND SCIENCE and DEPARTMENT OF HEALTH AND SOCIAL SECURITY (1978) Coordination of services for children under five. LA Social Services Letter LASSL (78) 1 Health Notice HN (78) 5. DES Reference S47/24/013.

FROEBEL, F. (1887) *The Education of Man*. London: Appleton.

GARVEY, C. (1977) *Play*. London: Fontana/Open Books; Cambridge, Massachusetts: Harvard University Press.

GINSBERG, S. (1976) Women, work and conflict. In *Mothers in Employment*. London: Brunel University Management Programme and Thomas Coram Research Unit. 75–89.

JOLLY, H. (1975) *Book of Child Care*. London: Allen & Unwin.

McMILLAN, M. (1921) *The Nursery School*. London: Dent.

MINISTRY OF HEALTH (1945) Circular 221/45.

MONTESSORI, M. (1912) *The Montessori Method*. London: Heinemann.

PINCHBECK, I. and HEWITT, M. (1973) *Children in English Society*. London: Routledge & Kegan Paul; Toronto: University of Toronto Press.

PRESCOTT, E. (1973) A comparison of three types of day care and nursery school – home care. Paper presented at the Biennial Meeting of the Society for Research in Child Development. Philadelphia. 29 March–1 April 1973.

PRESCOTT, E. and JONES, E. (1971) Day care for children. *Children*. March–April 1971.

RAYNES, N., PRATT, M. and ROSES, S. (1977) Aides' involvement in decision-making and the quality of care in institutional settings. *American Journal of Mental Deficiency*. **81**, 570–77.

ROBERTSON, J. (1958) *Young Children in Hospital*. London: Tavistock.

RUTTER, M. (1972) *Maternal Deprivation Reassessed*. Harmondsworth and New York: Penguin.

SPOCK, B. (1955) *Baby and Child Care*. New York: Hawthorne; London: Bodley Head.

TIZARD, J., MOSS, P. and PERRY, J. (1976) *All Our Children*. London: Temple Smith/New Society.

TRADES UNION CONGRESS WORKING PARTY (1976) *The Under Fives*. London: TUC.

YUDKIN, S. (1967) *0–5: a Report on the Care of Preschool Children*. London: National Society of Children's Nurseries.

Index

128 **INDEX**

Other titles from the Oxford Preschool Research Project

Jerome Bruner

Under Five in Britain

'It does not take deep probing to recognize that the modern family is beset by difficulties in finding the care outside the home that parents feel they need. The difficulties arise not within the family but in the broader community – they are economic, social, and political, but their impact on the life of children is personal, value-laden and highly controversial.'

Much is known about the need for full- or part-time care away from home. Well-planned experience stretches under-fives and gives them confidence for school ahead. Parents also need the break: depression has been shown to be widespread among young mothers constantly at home. Increasingly, financial need sends both parents to work, and for single parents the pressures are still more harsh. The fact is that the workforce has grown in recent years largely by recruiting younger women.

In the face of clear need, what form should preschool provision take? This book presents a searching appraisal of what is currently available, and uses the evidence of the Oxford Preschool Project to show how far the kinds of care on offer – nursery schooling, playgroups, childminding, and day nurseries – can be said to succeed in their separate attempts to provide for the nation's under-fives. There is no doubt that fundamental improvements are needed, and that government initiative must lead the way. Professor Bruner discusses the options open at a time of economic stringency. He argues that the reluctance of successive governments to respond to preschool need fails the present generation and sets the next at risk.

Kathy Sylva, Carolyn Roy and Marjorie Painter

Childwatching at Playgroup and Nursery School

'What colour's that?'
'Red.'
'No, dear.'

What is the point of playgroups and nursery schools? Most would agree that play speeds children's intellectual development and other children's company improves social confidence. But the evidence is that only certain sorts of play excite children and stretch their capacities, and only some kinds of social exchange add to what is on offer at home. Too much time on pastry shapes, too much getting heard above the noise, too many adult led activities, really waste the preschool opportunity. So what are the activities that bring present and future benefit, and how are they likely to be fostered?

Analysing several hundred hours of systematic observation, this book shows clearly how the structure of preschool time and setting drastically affects the gain that children can make from their experience. Nor are its findings relevant only to British under-fives: parallel studies in Oxfordshire and Miami draw the same conclusions from very different kinds of preschool provision. Those conclusions have immediate practical value for any playleader or teacher of the very young.

Three appendices show how research techniques developed on this project can be – and are being – applied to individual playgroups and nursery classes.

'Yesterday was my birthday,' said Mrs Jones. 'I'm five and Jason's three,' responded Susan, 'I'm older than Jason and older than Midget.' 'Who's Midget?' 'She's the cat and we found her in the shed and she had kittens . . . five of them and they're all black . . . except one's ginger.'

Bridget Bryant, Miriam Harris and Dee Newton

Children and Minders

'He's very withdrawn – you'll take that back to the office and say it's because he's minded but it's not. He worries about his father hurting his mother or his baby sister – I don't know what to say to him. He also rocks and head bangs but not so much here now. He needs lots of reassurance – to be told I love him. He's fiercely independent and tries not to show his feelings – it's terrible in a child that age.'

Of all forms of child care, minding is currently and most controversial. On the one hand, the Departments of Education and of Health and Social Security praise its 'home-like' quality, and hope to make good its admitted shortcomings in a spirit of 'low cost realism'. On the other hand, recent research has focused on the damaging conditions in which some children are minded, especially in the inner cities.

Against this background, the authors examine childminding of perhaps the highest standard it is reasonable to expect. They look in detail at the lives and expectations of minders, and of mothers who need their services, and they discuss the relationships that grow between the two. They ask how far minders can really provide a home from home, and to what extent the Social Services provide adequate back-up. But chiefly they focus on the experience of the children themselves, and it is here that their findings give cause for serious concern; certainly a third and possibly a half of the children now being minded are failing to thrive, and some could be disturbed; and this is for reasons largely unconnected with the minders' qualities or qualifications. It is plainly not enough to expand and improve the childminding service; it is vital that means be found to locate the children who need quite different provision, and to ensure that they have it.

Grant McIntyre Limited specializes in social, behavioural and medical science, and publishes books of all kinds – introductory and advanced texts, handbooks and reference works, practical manuals, and important research. Our aim is to make a continuing wealth of new work available to all readers for whom it has value.

Look for our books at your local bookshop, or write for a catalogue or to order direct simply fill in the form below, and list the books you want.